CW01480999

Cracked, Maybe? …but not Crumbled

By
Marie Parnes

Spinetinglers Publishing
www.spinetinglerspublishing.com

Spinetinglers Publishing

22 Vestry Road, Co. Down

BT23 6HJ, UK

www.spinetinglerspublishing.com

First published by Spinetinglers Publishing, 3rd July 2012.

ISBN: 978-1-906755-16-4

Printed in the United Kingdom

"There had to be more to life! So I set out to find it. A wonderful song, "Follow Me" gave me the courage to follow as God led me.

My journey encouraged two ladies to get out of the box, which motivated me to write this book. Hopefully, as with these two ladies it will encourage you too."

MARIE PARNES

"Few people make a lasting impression on you, like Marie does!

She will charm your smile from you. Her wisdom is apparent, while her kindness and generosity are the basis of her humour.

Read on and experience what it means to live through her words, allowing them to draw you into adventures."

MPHO MTIMKULU (PAUL)

"Marie (as in biscuit) is a fascinating, compelling character with a wicked sense of humour, a fighter for righteousness with a *BIG HEART.* There's always room for one more person and time for one more thing for Marie to fit into her busy schedule. If it's for God and for his people Marie always has time! *Cracked, Maybe? ...but not Crumbled* is a wonderful title for her first remarkable, hilarious story… An absolute must read!"

RED HUGHES

"You serve your function as a catalyst perfectly, sometimes without even realising it. I love you loads for being the life changing person you are."

ALEXANDER PARNES

Marie's book *Cracked, Maybe?...but not Crumbled* is one of encouragement! The title surely says it all.

The book is full of everyday life experiences which show that life is what you make it and that with God, there is always light at the end of the tunnel.

In this book is the story of Marie's life. It is one of determination, resilience and with a 'let's get on with it attitude'. Marie's wittiness, matter of fact personality, love and care for her fellow human plus her evangelistic streak make the book a very interesting read.

Her exceptionally unique life experiences give hope to all who have been through the mill and are still hanging on despite the odds. Marie does life with enthusiasm, optimism and an ever ablaze vision! Indeed as the saying rightly goes, 'where there is a will, there is a way' does truly reflect her. For Marie the door will always open so long as you keep knocking.

It is my prayer that many will find the faith, hope and comfort that Marie has and gives as they read this book.

PAT MENSAH
JOY CHRISTIAN CENTRE INT. LONDON

PREFACE

His eyes darted in her direction. Uncomfortably pulling up his trousers, by the buckle of the belt, groaning in tightness, as it was holding up a growing concern of a beer belly!

What AM I doing here? I pondered, downing the last mouthful of my fish, chips, green peas with tea special, provided by the well-run local pub on the High Street.

I suddenly felt very vulnerable and too tired for any eye contact games with an overweight man, his dubious woman companion in tow. I had chosen the table in the far corner, hoping, as a woman eating on my own, it would be just that, left in peace, with my fragmented life to contemplate and the unfinished manuscript slowly taking shape into a proposed book! What had I written?

My autobiography! Setting the record straight, so to speak to all and sundry, who had varied views of my life over the years. Rather like people who observe a road accident at a four way stop street, arguing out the way the accident took place.

My nearest and dearest thought, sometimes, that I was just an accident, waiting for a place to happen! Whereas there were the faithful few who deemed me worthy to keep in prayer and really believed in me, witnessing how God lead me. I had always felt I was different. Was not sure how or why, but did - considered a child prodigy, I soon became an idol in my immediate family. As I grew older I found I had competition, as the property in Umtentweni, was an idol in itself! Becoming a Jesus fanatic! To finally resorting to being a single mum, after an exhausting seven-year marriage. Now after almost twenty years on my own of achieving goals, in work and ministry, that was growing sum what, moving to foreign lands to do assignments unknown for God. I had, had visions of things God had shown me too enormous, to possibly contemplate on my own surely. As a woman, I had felt lonely and asked God for a partner in marriage therefore ministry, wanting to feel more complete and fulfilled. Had I really flipped? Having announced that I was to remarry - a man almost half my age! If they thought I, could not be put in a box, they now had to try and fathom how two jacks-out-of-the boxes were going to pull whatever off. My new unconventional husband, causing havoc mostly, it seemed, and concern to all, wherever we went. I trying to hold onto any shred of respectability left, threw caution to the wind, and settled for God's opinion, not man!

Never mind, I believed I could see the bigger picture. Praise God for all that I consider real friends. They have faithfully prayed through satanic, witch and death attacks. The call has to be great, to have such a great attack!

I trust that my testimony, how to follow God and overcome, will encourage others to have the courage to get up and go, as He calls each one into full time service.

GOD BLESS

Marie Parnes

marieparnes@hotmail.com

Friends......
I have some wonderful friends....
Friends are like biscuits....
Some are very sweet.....
Some are slightly cheesy......
Some are getting out of date....
Some are just plain crackers....lol
Some thoughts from them about me.....

*I dedicate this book to the wonderful Friends,
Pastors and Prophets who have encouraged, taught
and guided me.*

HIGH DIVING IS NOT ONLY FOR THE BIRDS!!

When I read Psalm 80 that King David wrote in the Bible, I got the impression that I was to leave the bank. I was not particularly happy with my job, despite the success of leading a lunch time Christian meeting for staff… I'm sure that no-one, let alone myself, could read into it that God was telling me to leave the relative safety of the bank. I had answered an advert for a Christian book supplier that needed a travelling representative. Having even contemplated this made me realise I was ready for a change, in any direction. My daughter Kerry had worked at a Christian bookshop for her school work experience and triumphantly returned one day with an advert for a sales lady at that shop. Taking the plunge I went for the interview and got the job!

Well I believed it then and hence putting all my trust in the LORD (or was it my own logic?) I put the necessary months' notice in the beginning of November to leave the end of that month, as not only did the bank pay Christmas bonuses at the end of November, but my new job needed my services as a saleslady from 1st December. Although a drop in salary, the lonely 45 minute drive didn't deter me, I'd most definitely miss the lift club ladies chatter, we were friends for years and still years to come!

Excitedly seeing potential, not only to serve customers, but possibly counselling opportunities. The manager, a smiling golden redhead, with patience taught me as fast as he could all I needed to know. The annual Christmas sale of kids and Sunday School books due, a lot of work with stock needed to be counted, marked at reduced rates and advertising this weeks event! This shop was the last to go online and despair filled me. Thinking I had left the dratted computers back at the bank and now I had to learn a new system to boot!! Excuse the pun!!

It had been discussed that I was to go north to the shop in Johannesburg for one month to learn the new system. The trials through that time was not easily got through. Almost regretting that I thought I had heard God in this move, that my spirit of adventure always to the ready was challenged to say the least in this call to duty! The highlight was staying with my dear friend Bettie, a past Telefriend counsellor colleague of mine. The distance between Pretoria where Bettie lived and the shop in Johannesburg proved too exhausting physically and financially with bumper-to-bumper traffic. In the mornings I saw red tail lights glaring like monsters trudging to a secret destination, on the way home with the night lights of the vehicles switched on, it was a gentle diamond necklace effect, stretched car after car along the concrete highway. Another friend had a friend, Brenda and family, who lived closer to

Johannesburg, and kindly allowed me to come and stay for the remainder of my time at the shop, enveloping me and my daughter, Kerry, who came to hear Rodney Howard Browne convention held at Midrand, nearby.

I had still worn my old wedding ring, although divorced for many years, call it safety from any unwanted suitors, and/or having to deal with any lingering undisturbed emotions! There were so many needing prayers that were stretched out throughout the auditorium, as the Holy Spirit touched people, some going down like dominos, some laughing, some crying as they were ministered to individually. Myself, laying on the carpeted floor, got a vision of how God saw me - in a glass casket as if I was dead, waiting to be buried, or kissed awake by my beloved, as was Snow White.

I heard the words Jesus used to Jariuses's daughter "Arise, damsel, arise."

Suddenly I was on my feet, trying to rip my wedding ring off, that had in love caused me so much pain and sorrow in my marriage. Tears falling, I said to Kerry, "Come with me," rushing off to the ladies powder room, soaping my fourth finger, got the now offending ring off and gave it to her as a memory. A new sort of life seemed to flood me, and recognising God's purpose for me being upcountry, was not just for work, but for healing and hope in trusting Him for the future.

Imagine my surprise on my return to Durban, to find my manager friend GONE! Now what? Talk that the shop was in the red and the possibility of closing very real. I stood my ground against the Devil and whoever else was involved, as it was my suspicion that the head manageress had not being happy with my employment by Alan anyway. I had not misheard God surely? Two months out of my bank job, and with new employment rules in place, I had been warned that there would be little or no chance of getting my old job back if my new job did not work out when I left, so now what? God must have a plan and I was going to find it whatever it was…

No confirmation that the shop was indeed closing, or that I was now unceremoniously the new "BOSS" and with no increase of salary either! Another stock take due, time wise I knew I could not achieve by due date, so roped my daughter and her friend to help me get the job done successfully. To my horror found that much stock had been lying idle on the shelves for years, and not much new stock able to be purchased through lack of funds! "What should I do God?"

The best I could come up with, as ALL good things come from God above. The thought dropped into my spirit '*have a sale, and with the money buy new stock*'... this had to be God!

With my artistic skills I drew up a SALE flyer, photocopied by the score, put them in the customer's packets. In faith I found out who the book and music suppliers were, and fortunately found that the book suppliers were in my city the next week, so invited myself to the days event in a posh hotel with delicious eats and drinks throughout the day, and had a wonderful time choosing and ordering new uplifting contemporary books! The Sarepta music suppliers sent their representative, Allan, around for me to view all the latest Gospel music available. Allan turned out to be the brother of our keyboard player at my church, which made business much friendlier. Never mind that the head lady complained at how much money was spent on my latest expedition.

"Victory is mine," says the Lord, which I clung to as the atmosphere in the bookshop changed. Days passed pleasantly until I got a dreadful phone call from the "head lady" who was yelling at me for whatever I was supposed to have done wrong… couldn't quite think what I had done that was so bad to get such a grilling. As I had a shop full of people, old customers and new, thanks to my sale that had gone off extremely well, I pulled the telephone out of its socket and got on with what I seem to do best, serving people.

At the close of day, holistically satisfied with the way issues on all levels had been dealt with and the fat takings safely locked away, I suddenly remembered to plug the phone back in to its socket, immediately it rang, and my heart sank expecting another tirade. Warily I answered.

"Marie speaking."

"MARIE," the whispered urgency in the little bookkeeper's voice was strained. "Do you know why 'she' was so mad earlier and trying to fault you?"

"No!" I replied, not really interested, as after a successfully tiring day, all I had done was obey God and do my work to His Glory.

"Well you have made 37,000 Rand profit and your shop has done more sales than 'her' shop and your shop will not have to close down!!"

Thank you Jesus, to God be the Glory, singing the old time favourite "Trust and Obey" all the way home, proving you can't have a testimony, without a test as the saying goes…

The battle was not over by far as the head manageress determinedly put an advert out for a new manager/manageress. I found out when a lovely lady named Yvonne arrived one day for an interview with some bigwigs from Head Office. As I am prophetic god gave me a revelation that was sin in the camp so to speak.

1. That someone in leadership of this Christian organisation was also a freemason. (A sect that worships Satan unknowingly.)
2. That in the book of Malachi it says that employers that pay their workers low/unfair wages have a curse on them.

I was to speak to a man called Brian. Little did I know that a Brian was coming from afar, to be part of the interview for Yvonne. I gave her the tip to hang in, to get the higher wage due and not accept the wage I had had to be satisfied with. She got her wage, but not before I was able to challenge Brian and co. beforehand. Yvonne became my senior and friend, as we settled amicably into the daily routine, teaching her all I knew, greatly relieved to give the dratted computer duties over to Yvonne's superior knowledge. My yoke is easy my burden is light came to me. Due to a now buzzing business, we were able to purchase a lovely Victorian home to be our new shop in a more accessible, affluent part of the city and nearer for me to drive to work, cutting my petrol costs, thank you Lord!!

From offering to drop off some new bibles for an elderly customer, who was housebound, I made a dear friend in Doreen Shickerling who was then 84 years old. Who had through her life turned her hand to anything she could use her skills at from teaching to managing the city operas years long ago, to radio and at that point, still studying and earning degrees annually, for theology and masters in Greek, to name a few accolades she received by 90 years old. Her encouragement, amongst many others, for me to set pen to paper, must take credit for what you now read, as I would regale her and others with testimonies of my seemingly haphazard lifestyle.

As a single parent with funds stretched to a premium, I put any talents inherited from my late mother to use to earn an extra bit of cash here and there. Juggling a full day job at the bank, then the bookshop, sang in operas and musicals at night, singing at weddings where I usually decorated the wedding cake, and helped with the catering! Did my share of Telefriend, telephone counsel duties, helped run the music team at church and did my best to be involved in my daughter's school activities.

All the spare money received for these interests were used to be able to enjoy brief breakaways somewhere. For one holiday we travelled up the coast to Bonamanzi, (means look at the water) a game reserve, as we could not afford the plush cottages we stayed in a tree house for the minimal fee. What fun to have the view from our treetop vantage point as animals wandered lazily munching below our lofty rooms high in the trees. Our shower was an experience, as there were HUGE moths and spiders that lead to much wonder and then screaming as they moved and fluttered around Kerry's friends's heads, they were included in on the adventure while their mother went on honeymoon. At night there was another flurry of fear as the "Nagappies" (night monkeys), with the faint moonlight shining on their big golden eyes, stared down at us through the cracks at the top of the door of our 'room.' Everyone wanted to sleep in my room for safety, as these little animals had scared them half to death, talk of witchdoctors and such were soon squashed as a torch shone on their furry faces proved not so!

Even though I can remember going to Sunday School at the age of 3 years old and until 23 years old, I very naively thought everyone knew about Jesus, and that everyone died and went to heaven! At 23 I really came to understand the real "Born Again" salvation! I had gone to an evangelistic outreach from the Logos ship. This ship was one of three known as The Mercy Ships, hospital ships that give free hospital care for third world countries. When the call came at the end of the meeting to come and join and serve on the ship, excitement leapt in me, to deflate as quickly thinking what my family would say? I could just imagine! "Whoever heard of such a thing, you must be crazy, stay in your nice secure job at the bank." At Grandpa's funeral some time later I heard the words "let the dead bury the dead" but as a young Christian and wrapped up with grief, I did not know that it was a scripture and continued with "and follow me." Years later with hindsight, it was the first costly BIG lesson to NOT have fear of man's opinion, to teach others to not have to live with regret of not taking that high dive of trust and get Gods possible perfect will for my life and not the permissive will, which has been up till now interesting but may have been so different.

Hence nearly twenty years later, when the flagship of the Mercy Ships, the Anastasis, was docking for repairs in the east coast harbour of East London, South Africa, and calling for volunteers to help while full time or long-term staff could have a holiday break! Guess who felt the pull again to go? They needed anyone who would be the hands and heart of Jesus as their famous saying goes. Everyone on board from eye surgeons to deck hands, all paid the fee charged and served willingly.

Kerry knowing of my lost dream, urged me to apply along with her application. We were both accepted, to our delight. Even though the ship was not leaving the port and we were going to melt in the bowels of the ship in the heat of the South African summer. It was exciting serving Jesus with a difference! As one had to book the dates you could serve and I was overdue my two weeks annual leave at the book shop, the holiday pay would be just enough to pay for myself, so went ahead and booked!

I had a vision of me on a high diving board and being pushed off and forced to dive into the pool, and as I went down I noticed a white edge around the pool and heard the lord say "this was your training ground" and on entering the water, and on coming up for air, looked around and saw I was in open sea, which I knew was a call to the nations. Direction at last, not thinking it might not happen as quickly as I would like it to be.

Shortly after this vision Doreen Schikerling phoned me to say God had given her a Psalm 27 for me, which said I should not fear my enemies. Ten minutes later, Brenda, whom I had stayed with in Johannesburg, phoned me to say she had a prophetic word for me, "The Lord says even though the water does not always come out the tap, the well is not dry."

What did that mean? I wondered, *What was God saying?*

The overall manageress seized her chance to upset my plans, by not agreeing with my dates booked with the ship. After several attempts to reconcile dates to no avail I called on a senior member of the board whose daughter, unbeknown to be, had also served at YWAM, the mission school, , therefore sympathetic to my cause, granted my leave request! Just before leaving for my adventure, the inevitable phone call to try and ruin my joy, "If you go, I will fire you!"

"You do what you have to do and I will do what I have to do," was my quick reply.

I suddenly could imagine how the three Hebrew boys felt standing their ground before being thrown into the fire, and here I was with my faith really being tested! If God be God then you serve Him was my response to people that questioned my wisdom in this faith move! Standing your ground when finances are not good at the best of times, now to be suddenly out of work with bills to pay, made me phone Kerry, who was already in her time on the ship, paid by kind courtesy of her father, to say maybe I should wait to come, as I would need that cash to pay to keep her until she went to the YWAM mission school (oh ye of little faith). My heart sank for the first time at the enormity of the results of my decision!

Kerry was very upset for me and went to obediently tell the personnel lady of the change, once again!

OK GOD this is the deal, IF you can get someone to pay for my two weeks on board, I can cope with the bus fare and pocket money necessary for the long cool drinks that had to be purchased, that I had been warned I would need. Just when it's darkest my Heavenly father comes through, picks me up and tells me it will be alright. Kerry phoned later to say that the personnel lady and her husband had prayed and felt lead to pay for my time on the boat! Mission accomplished! God and I have been making these sort of deals ever since only they keep getting bigger… God is so able to teach us so gently to learn to trust Him.

It was a sticky, hot precarious bus drive down to East London, through the Eastern Cape, little did I know that journey would be the first of many, in years to come. On board the staff had kindly taken my age into consideration, and settled me into a cabin by myself. I was devastated not to be in with people from around the world who I wanted to get to know. Until God, through circumstances, showed me I needed the solitude, as there were a few full time workers that needed encouraging, and I could not have had that liberty in a cabin full of jolly young people, so once again God had things under control.

I was delegated to the housekeeping department and for the first few days I cried on and off, eventually I went to Linda, my senior, about my tears. She chuckled, explaining that many went through the same emotions, as genuine humility overcame each, and the corporate anointing was filling, healing people who were at the right place at the right time.

This time there were 400 on board and 33 nations represented, all loving and serving Jesus, and the whole ship worshipping was awesome… sadly the time came to an end too quickly. Not before my department's outreach into the city I met a lady called Leslie, who valiantly helped her mother with a women's street ministry. Leslie had separated from her husband, due to money becoming his God through favour in business. She had decided to study psychology to help the one son that had problems. On board one night I had ministered to a little Philippine lady whose son had similar problems. This boy needed special tests and assessments, that neither she nor her husband could afford. This information came with spending prayerful time with her until four in the morning! I quickly invited Leslie to meet her when the ship hosted a barbeque for the volunteers. Leslie approached her professor and a free session set up for the boy. Thank you Jesus!! I prayed much for Leslie's broken marriage and after nearly two months Leslie phoned me excitedly - her husband had repented, they were getting remarried on the original date of their first marriage, and he was coming back to his East London business and had purchased a house that had extra cottage for her parents provided. God's faithfulness proved once again.

Back in Durban, after a weary 18 hour bus journey, I started packing up the dear little flat Kerry and I had shared. We moved back down the coast, to the old family farm style house built by my grandfather many years previously. Unhealthy living boarders, land rate expenses, an old toilet that incessantly went wrong and no real funds to fix it long term, added to the problems. I was determined to follow through with what was, I believed, the next step for Kerry and myself - to proceed to the YWAM Mission School in the Cape. Numerous

Marie Parnes

phone calls and arrangements later completed, and Kerry was off. Her father, Barry, kindly agreed to pay for her 6th course. God is so good!

It was not so easy for me, and I believed God was making sure I knew He was my guide and provider. So the deal I set to God was 'you show me for sure you want me at YWAM, by providing a ticket to Cape Town.'

I had not managed to raise much sponsorship, and YWAM had agreed to subsidize the difference, which left me once again needing money for transport.

I woke that Friday morning with an urgency in my spirit that I could to get there by the Sunday registration. I drove to see a friend of long standing through my stage career, Jan, who owned the local travel agent in my hometown, to ask if she would sponsor me anything. I might as well think BIG... how about a plane ticket I enthused, hoping she would catch the urgency. Calm as always, even today, bless you Jan for your longsuffering with me.

"Go look on my staff computer and see if there are any places on the buses going down." There were two seats left, in faith I said "I will take one," pulling my worn cheque book out with not much in it to brag about!

"Put that away," Jan waved her hand expressively. "The agency will take care of that."

I promptly burst into tears at the 11th hour deliverance.

"There, there," Jan tutted as I hugged her a grateful goodbye.

On return to the house, my aunty told me that the local pastor's wife had phoned, and that someone was prepared to pay for my ticket to Cape Town. God was making sure I was getting to Mission School no matter who obeyed! For years aunty and I had haggled over the issues of the property as co-owners, up to that point she would never agree to anything that would benefit us, which made life for both of us very difficult. Now she was following me around as I packed my case to the brim. (One never knew where God was leading me after the course.)

"What must I do with the property?" she said over again as the morning progressed.

"I don't care, I am sick of being controlled and blamed with anything to do with it, so I'm going to follow Jesus, just DON'T lose my inheritance!"

Prophetic words indeed!

The longer bus journey further south was exhausting, through the hot dry Karoo desert, the road winding its way eventually through majestic mountain passes and green vineyards of the wine making district of the southern Cape, towards Cape Town.

Kittie, a staff member kindly fetched me in her car. How you managed to show me servant hood, carrying my laden suitcase up the stairs to my neat welcoming room, to be shared with one other. Kittie, I salute you, and that you still my friend amazing!

I still need help in keeping my luggage to a minimal. I was called a women for all seasons prophetically, so I try and be ready for all occasions, and it shows in my packing! My reasoning is God is a God of surprises, be prepared is my motto, not that those who help carry want to know!

God has really got a sense of humour, and knows just how to round all the rough and sharp edges off us. We want our own way, to do and go where we would, rather than where He knows is good for us.

While on the ship I, who did not really like housework, was spent my time cleaning toilets. Kerry, who kept everything in her room ship shape so to speak, and did not enjoy cooking much, was put to serve in the galley. Up at 4am, peeling dozens of pockets of veggies as the 400 on board needed her help to feed them.

God was deciding to continue working on our attitudes when we were sent to the mission centres. Kerry, who loves the beach and sea, was sent to Worcestor base at the foot of the mountains. Myself, who enjoys the mountains, having been brought up with the sea on my doorstep, was sent to the base at Muizenberg, the building practically on the beach! A few weeks previously I had a vision of an old sailing ship on a bay alongside mountains, and had wondered where that was. I had laughed as I could hear the creak of the old timber of the ship as it moved with the tide, and I said "Yes Lord, you have had to wait until I am older, more mature in You Lord, before you could send me out, I don't think I'm creaking but use me anyhow, anywhere".

I settled into my shared room, my roommate, was a dynamic, animated lady, called Elsabe. We were delighted with the gift of our own mug holding chocolate and welcome note, with a prophetic word about me having a heart of gold which was encouraging as I had some feeling of remorse with the 'hard' line I had seemingly taken with aunty.

I decided to go for a walk to familiarize myself with my new surroundings. I first went to the tourist information, a few minutes' walk away, to see what was of interest that would not cost me money to see. I only had 50 Rand for my pocket money, which had to last 3 months. Not anything free, disappointed I turned to leave the centre and gasped, as there was a big carved ship just like I had seen in my vision with its sails up. As I walked over to the beach side of the road I noticed the bay, with the mountains meeting, just like my vision. I now had no doubt that I was in God's will at Mission School.

The lectures were enjoyably of value, and I surprised myself and fellow students when marked with an A+ for my morning devotion presentation, that we each took in turn. My cooking skills noted, I happily headed up the main evening meal, which once even received a round of applause when I changed some mundane ingredients into something creative. I helped the Chinese couple who headed up the soup kitchen for street people, which was appreciated. I also became firm friends with an American lady, Pat, who headed up evangelism in my Muizenburg base. I visit her periodically when I'm in the area where she has settled near Durban, helping with the rural folk and their needs.

A prophet used as a catalyst in numerous situations was not always appreciated, and as I had struggled with a persistent cough at the start of the course, my pocket money dwindled rapidly, as I bought all sorts to suppress or fix my cough. With many prayers later, accused of maybe having demons even, I got trotted off to the nearest hospital where an old missions doctor chuckled and said I was allergic to the pollen season, which was all over, making the cape a beautiful sight to see as spring was heralded in.

In one of my weekends off and not feeling great, I took to my bed! The team due to cook for the evening meal did not even know how to light the gas cooker, let alone get it together to cook for the hungry group coming back from outdoor activities. I got a telling off for being in the kitchen bare foot to help them, as they had constantly begged for my help. I noted that not one staff member that was on duty for weekends was around! That got soon rearranged as I took my suggestions to the young man Johan, who headed the base.

I had also visited Kerry's base another weekend, a 2 hour drive away. I took note that the spiritual atmosphere was a lot clearer than over Muizenburg. There were Freemasons, and plenty of satanic activity, with added issues from the people of all nations at the school, coming with their superstitions and problems. I suggested that they try and move the head base to Worscestor. I am happy to report it took time but Y.W.A.M was able to purchase the old hospital in that town and has been running as a base successfully since.

Due to my exposing Jezabel in the woman who was in charge of the school, she refused to let me get further sponsorship to do the outreach section of the course. Having no money just before the school closed, it was surprised to have an early Christmas card sent by my cousin, with 10 Rand inside. As my hair needed a cut, I desperately scoured the town for a hairdresser in my price range. The last one I called at happened to give YWAM'ers discount and I happily paid up, and left feeling refreshed and looking smart for the up and coming Christmas banquet.

This dinner was so special, as every nation represented, made a traditional national dish, and dressed up in national costume for the occasion. To make it more special, my daughter, Kerry was coming to stay and partake, before leaving for home. Home was far away and I had to trust God again for my return fare. My dear friend, Elsabe came to the rescue and offered to pay my fare home in exchange for travelling the long route to get to her town, as she wanted company. Arriving in Durban, I was met by a friend, who had the use of my car while I was away.

Back home with the bank loan for my car to repay, I looked for work locally. I managed to get a part-time job at the Kwikspar bakery, getting the staff evangelized and giving out bibles, which rattled the Hindu boss, who made life trying at times. This added to the fact that my cough got worse with the inconstant temperatures of work.

I decided to go to the local hospital for a check-up, where the ancient doctor on attendance said glibly, "you've got a bit of throat cancer, we will operate, a bit of chemotherapy and you should be fine."

When he wrote down that the right tonsil had to come out, when it was the left one, I started questioning his diagnosis - if he did not know his left from his right, what else need I question? Was the doctor really talking about me? It seemed as if I was to be the bearer of bad news for someone else.

***

As Kerry was away as a leader on yet another church kids camp I phoned her to ask her support through this. She, along with other friends, were so upset, as everyone enjoyed my singing and the one question on everyone lips, was would I be able to sing again… I prayed so.

Kerry told a dear friend, EV, who had been like a mother to many of us who needed her help in one way or another. EV phoned to invite me up to Durban, now years later, was only an hours' drive away, for a second opinion at mission run hospital… It was confirmed! We both sat and cried! The growths all the way down my throat were to be removed with my tonsils, that looked like rotten plums.

Having had several operations in my life, and never having an adverse effect from the anaesthetic, I was gagging on the hour every hour. The Devil was still trying to silence me, or even get rid of me. I fell asleep at one stage of the night, but woke up with the sound of the death rattling in my ears, chocking on my vomit. I heard the Spirit of the Lord say, 'Come against the Spirit of Infirmity, Death and Hell in the Name of Jesus.' As I did this, my voice shouted out loud, "in the Name of Jesus," disturbing the ward. Only then, was I given an injection. The gagging stopped, and slept like a babe until morning. On waking I ate a full breakfast. That the orange juice stung my throat, did not deter me as others in the ward asked for prayer as they faced their operations. I awaited one or both of the surgeons's news, at last the younger one came to my bedside.

"Marie, you know all those growths we saw down your throat?"

I waited with bated breath.

"Well," he continued, "we went right down to your voice box."

Fear gripped me for a moment. *would I be able to sing ever again?* I wondered to myself.

A very puzzled look came over him. "We couldn't find any growths, we removed the tonsils and performed a biopsy and will let you know if it's malignant or not."

"My God does not do half a job of healing people, the results will be not malignant!" I said with utter confidence. To the young man's embarrassment and the amusement of the onlooking ward, I made him give me a high five hand salute for Jesus.

Now I was of even greater interest, and some were confessing their faith in Jesus. Before going into hospital, I had watched a Bennie Hinn programme on the TV and as he was praying, through word of knowledge he said, "there is someone with throat cancer and God is healing you now!"

It could have been anyone in the whole world, but I said Lord, "I receive my healing today, thank you Father." I had my church, family and friends also praying… I had stood my ground against the enemy.

Since this experience, fighting the Spirit of Death and Hell, I have discovered that with most people that have nasal, throat and bronchial chest problems, it's THIS SPIRIT one has to come against, besides any other emotional issues binding the people. I had my South African friend Pat tell me she had a vision of me on high ground, blowing a trumpet at my mouth. An Anglican minister, I met, said when he prayed for me he was given Ishiah 58 v 1 – 'Raise your voice like a trumpet and tell my people their sins.'

As a Prophet, catalyst and straight talker, I have had to learn to season my words strictly or as gently as deemed necessary, I'm often as popular a pork chop in a synagogue. As long as I get the job done is the most important thing, so God gets Glory. We have been made to worship him and I still continue to sing, teaching folk to enter the high praises, worship in fullness and allowing freedom to come as the Lord. The Lord inhabits the praises of HIS people, the anointing comes down, breaking the yokes of the enemy, setting captives free. NOT MALIGNANT! TO GOD THE GLORY!

Marie and I go back 26 years. She loves the Lord with all her heart, and talks a lot, especially about God comes through for her. She has a heart of Gold, and will do anything to help a friend. I praise God she's is MY friend.

LYNN SKIDMORE

Marie Parnes is a survivor against all odds, her life is a testimony of God's faithfulness. Knowing Marie is a constant reminder to me that there must be a God! Blessings.

BERYL SMITH

ISRAEL – IT'S PAINFUL GROWING WINGS

After my recovery from the 'cancer' operation, one night I had cried to the Lord for my own finances, still feeling not particularly well, I fell asleep in a flood of tears… suddenly I woke up to a sweet aroma and fragrance of flowers filled the room! The word Lily of the Valley, Rose of Sharon sprung to mind, and I knew my Lord was with me. As I opened my eyes I could see the cream material of his garments, and in his hand was a cream satin drawstring pouch. His free hand opened the top and moved it so I could see inside as I was laying down. The bag was nearly full of gold coins. He dipped His hand in and gave me four of the coins. I said

"Thank you Lord, I know I will be alright now," and went peacefully back to sleep.

As work, and therefore salary eluded me, I contented myself to settle into a comfortable daily companionship with my dear friend Ev, an elder in our church who kindly let me stay. I made myself as useful as possible, helping out with shopping, cooking and babysitting grandchildren of various ages.

A Muslim lady, turned Christian, told her powerful testimony to me, and as I wanted to hear more I went to visit her at her little hair salon she had in her home. Some months previously my cousin Lynne had phoned me and suggested I go for an interview for a Nanny position in a posh suburb of Durban. I found the would-be employer to be a Muslim, me, a Christian, did not get the job. Here in my new friend's salon was the very same woman from the interview a year previously, having her hair done, and once again needing now a relief nanny for three weeks. I motioned to my friend that I wanted the job. It was suggested, and inwardly I chuckled, as either she really did not recognise me or didn't want to lose face with her hairdresser. It was agreed upon that I start a.s.a.p. Happily, I went off to tell Ev the good news.

Driving through the ornate electronic gate, I was welcomed with a huge house perched on high cliffs. With a magnificent view through massive glass windows, that overlooked the rocky beach and dazzling sea below and made me feel quite dizzy! The children, ranging from 8 years down to 16 months old, were of Turkish origin, spoilt rotten and had no discipline what so ever! There was opulence and obvious wealth, From snatches of conversation I got a distinct impression, that I'd rather not know the origins of the wealth. This was a taste of more to come, and be endured on this path God was leading me on.

The three weeks came to a close, not quickly enough for my liking. I was searching the employment section of the daily paper, and noticed an advert for a nanny in Cairo! Excitement rushed through me, Egypt, next to Israel, the land I had longed to visit, since my conversion, what an opportunity not to be missed! The small salary earned, covered the cost of getting the bus up to Johannesburg for the interview, which went well, and I was accepted. Until one lightning filled, stormy night, the lady employer from Cairo, a Muslim of course, phoned to say that the Egyptian government wanted her to employ an Egyptian and would not give her a work visa for me! CRASH, all my plans shattered and my meagre cash gone!

I could feel I was on a roll, sensing the nudge of the Holy Spirit wanting to move me out of comfort zones and South Africa, drawing me into deeper waters. It reminded of that vision I had of me bobbing in open sea. It was time to go!

Buying the Job Mail, an international newspaper, and running through it, an advert jumped out at me. Au Pairs were needed in Israel a.s.a.p, this was more like it, and I was in the age requirement. Just a phone call away, I found I needed my airfare of 3000 Rand and minimum 2000 Rand for pocket money to enable me to enter Israel. My car showing signs of wear and rust, would probably not fetch the princely sum needed, and if sold in haste, with selling price dropped, it would certainly not fetch the needed money! Ev kindly came to the rescue, lending me the full amount, with promise of repayment from me. I left my car in Kerry's care to sell, (that was my big mistake), to give Ev most of the cash back as soon as possible! Later down the line, I phoned Kerry to find my car had been sold for 800 Rand, I was furious to say the least, as I knew it could have brought at least a few thousand, so was yelling in frustration at my daughter on the phone from Israel, with her in tears, saying, "don't scream at me from another country!"

"YOU'RE jolly lucky I'm IN another country!" was my sharp retort.

I had not had the heart at that point to make her anxious for me, having lost my job, and did not know how I was indeed going to pay my friend back, let alone survive in Tel Aviv!

Anyway, once again my luggage bulging, my newly permed hair bobbing like big plums on top my head, by kind courtesy of Cheryl, hairdresser and friend from church, tears dried from hearing my daughter sing a solo she had written for me. Hugs and fond goodbyes were said at the Durban airport, I waved goodbye to the land below as the plane tilted upward. I settled in my seat, looking forward to my first Jewish meal on the El Al flight, that would initiate my taste buds for meals in my new 'home' for an unknown season.

On landing the interrogation of the customs officials at Ben Guerion Airport, Tel Aviv, was more stringent than the officers on leaving Johannesburg back in South Africa. Eventually, I was released to go to meet my host family, who were waiting in the foyer. A young, arrogant looking, Israeli man waited to greet me, holding a large card, with my name written in bold letters on it. His face fell as he saw me. I must have looked a sight bearing down towards him. I giggled to myself as I realized, that I, my luggage, or both was not what he was expecting. More like a petite 22 year old in high heels, and expectations of an affair, not likely! That indeed was a word of knowledge, as that's why myself, a safe middle-aged women was now employed.

Before leaving South Africa, my prophetic friend Pat had prayed with me and saw a vision of two polar bears, and said I would be going to a very cold country and feel isolated. Well, when I was presented with my set of keys to the apartment, the key ring had two polar bears on it! His wife, an American, held this explosive situation together somehow and gratefully handed me my 1 year old charge, who promptly screamed for her father. Thankfully, I busied myself in the kitchen, helping with a late dinner. After cleaning up, I got to bed at long last.

The father annoyingly stayed at home. A supposed unemployed lawyer, who made mission impossible to get close to the little girl. So, two weeks later I found myself, unemployed, unceremoniously dropped off at a seedy looking hostel near the beachfront, to have my first taste of hostel life with very little cash! The cosmopolitan travellers were unusual and friendly. To my delight a young man called Daniel from South Africa, joined this mixed bag of wannados. Over the first week I broke his façade of bravado down, he admitted he came from a Christian home and had rebelled by leaving, I soon had him repenting and recommitting his life to the Lord.

I had been asking God to show me if I was really in the right place, when a young Philippine girl asked me to go for a walk down the street with her that evening. We passed many interesting shops, and then a travel agent came to my attention, because in its display window was a large sailing ship made of thousands of matches. The ship vision was once again leading me, and peace flooded back to me again.

As the oldest member at the hostel, I surprised everyone, including myself, by fitting in so quickly. The receptionist, her loud golden blonde curls, out of a bottle of sorts with her mischievous smile was always a welcome sight. She spoke English, despite boasting a good Israeli name of Orna. Being of the same age, or there about, she occasionally, and kindly, took me out on her free time off in her car. Seeing the local sites, such as Jaffa with its picturesque harbour, I could picture the disciples fishing from there. There were hundreds of stairs to climb to the top, with little shops dotting the way up to where a large church dominated the plaza. Novel little shops with artistic ware for tourists to consider purchasing, and endless numbers of Change de Bureau, should one should need to change to dollars, the preferred currency other than the shekel. I learned to eat Humus, Gum'us and many local eastern delights, eating cheaply and filling you up.

I found the hostel to be a wealth of information, especially jobs and agents who had clients who needed people. I made my way to the Tel Aviv bus terminal, it was a six storey seething mass of people, scurrying to and fro to catch their buses on different levels of the building. I stopped briefly to buy a falafel filled with my choice, which was to die for, and a smoothie juice, concocted from my choice of fruit, to wash it down with - blended to satisfaction at a next to nothing price. Umpteen stalls, squashed together, with their sellers all shouting for attention, the noise was unbelievable. On hearing a favourite song of mine sung at a CD stall that sold fakes of every artist imaginable for only 10 shekels, I happily sang along and the owner was so impressed, gave me an extra CD for my effort.

Without any more dillydallying I made my way to the Job Shop, situated on the 4th floor of this organised mayhem. Delighted to have someone new on the books, I found myself employed and soon was ringing the doorbell of a five story luxury home in the district of Shookham Dan. The granny was lonely, fearful and suffering high blood pressure, hence she phoned her daughter at work constantly daily. Granny claimed she could not speak English, despite that I had found out that everyone learned English at school. She, I was told proudly, could speak five languages, so smiles and gestures were of the day as of course silly me, only spoke English!

What amazed me was that although requiring some help, they never thought to have a room prepared for you to sleep in. So, here in a house that each floor that looked out of Garden and Home magazine, or Hollywood, I was allocated the basement! It was the local dumping ground, and to my dismay after being sorted and cleaned, there was no bed, just a very clean cold tiled floor! I slept on a fancy sofa for two nights, then, was told triumphantly that my bed would be coming the next day. Every knock throughout the following day, was not my bed being delivered. At sunset the lady of the house arrived with a fold up canvas sunbed under her arm, gleefully saying, "here is your bed."

Dragging it to the cellar, down the many stairs, I was steaming at this acquisition, which from experience I knew was not much fun or comfort. The tiled floors in which are in every Israeli home, to cool the raging summer temperatures, did not cooperate, and my bed and I slid parting company, or folding up with me as a sandwich. In my frustration and exhaustion, working from sunrise to well past sunset, I burst into tears, with the huge puppy as witness, licking my tears and whining in sympathy!

I felt God saying, 'You go upstairs each morning, greeting with a smile, no matter how you feeling.' God knew how to teach me not to go on feelings. After I cleaned the whole house during the week, the woman had a Chinese man come in once a week and clean the whole house in one day. Was I mad to stay? No, just desperate to make enough money, firstly to pay Ev back and then to keep myself, and was just hanging in.

A month passed, and Orna faithfully fetched me most Saturdays away from my beautiful prison, as it had come to feel to me. The woman spitefully gave me Saturdays off, as due to Shabat, the Jewish Holy day, there was no public transport, only private transport was allowed. One day God showed me gold shining in Orna's hair... God was showing me that he saw her as special! I since have had other God show me gold on other people.

I was told that it had been decided to put Granny in an old age home, so I was not needed, not that I saw much of her, with all the house work expected of me aswell ascooking Granny's lunch and preparing supper for 8 p.m. I felt as if in a strange way the lady was trying to break me somehow. My choosing to keep the right attitude, had obviously got to her though. To my surprise, the day I packed to leave whilst waiting for Orna to lift me back to the hostel, to await a new assignment, the lady said, "Before you go, tell me why you are like you are?"

"Because I love Jesus Christ and love people."

"Really, tell me more," was her humbled reply.

I was able to explain how to become born again and challenged her on the prized bit of jewellery that wards off evil. It was distinctly turquoise blue, with a royal blue 'eye' in the centre, this glass object was set in gold, worn not only by superstition, that bound the wearer, but held them to idolatry, and therefore, their infirmities. 'My people perish through lack of knowledge,' was the scripture that sprung to mind. Understanding and freedom came, as I clarified the wiles of the devil. I was kindly given a warm coat to ward off the freezing cold, damp snow outside. My bulging case of South African summer wear was useless to fight the chill. Israel had the coldest winter in nine years, trust me to be there when it was below 0 degrees.

Jerusalem looked magnificent in white, as the snow lay thick from the parapets of the wall around her, stretching down to the Church of the Nations and Garden of Gethsemane in the valley below. Trudging in the snow with my luggage looking for a bed at any hostel was a task not for the faint hearted. The winding thin 'roads' throughout some areas of the walled city were a feat at the best of times.

Finding a hostel with a spare bed, high up in the old city, I clambered up the sharp angular steps inside the hostel, which were hewn in the stone cliff, they had been white originally, but were now a dirty opaque grey tinge from years of bodies and luggage wending their way up and down. The rooms had high conical cave like ceilings, a cold metallic frame held a typical double bunk beds together. The paper thin grey, army style blankets, had seen better days. They were folded neatly, lying on the hard Kauai mattresses, with springs poking out at angles. A thin woman, dressed in black, with worn black lace mantilla covering her straggly long black hair that could have used shampoo I feared, held a sombre, lone Shabbat vigil over three candles, flickering bravely at the lack of oxygen in the room. Between mumbles of prayer, she rapidly consumed a large bottle of red wine, blew out the candles, and fully clothed collapsed in bed until morning.

A South African female joined my freezing misery. As it was only half way through Shabat there was still no public transport to return to Tel Aviv. The Job Shop for my next assignment, sought out the only liquor store open and bought the same as the old lady. Sharing it added a spark of fun to the dreary cold weekend, lulling us off to sleep... not that it is the recommended sleeping potent, but trying to be spiritual had not helped!

Old Jerusalem became my firm favourite place to spend my off time in, seeping in the atmosphere of those days long ago. One night I had a dream of men wearing long cream capes, walking two by two down the stairs in the old city. 'What was that all about?' I wondered, as on waking the scene never left me. The fact that the city is divided up into religious belief sections interested me, and I had a few interesting encounters with all faiths - Christian, Arabic, Muslim and Jewish! On returning to the Agency, I noticed some special post cards at a shop next door in the Bus Station. They were to mark the Millennium year of 2000, and one card had that very scene on it. It was a religious event of some importance, once a year! I was so excited at this find, and an answer to my question!

Getting off the bus, the wind swirling the sand up to greet me, I was back at the airport to be picked up by my new assignment. A large ample bosomed, ruddy faced woman, with a warm smile and twinkling blue eyes, that watered all on their own, walked towards me. "Mori, welcome to

Israel!" Giving me a hug, she grabbed some of my luggage helpfully, and guided me through waiting people to her car. It was in a worse condition than mine had been, dust everywhere, and had seen better days. My new boss's logic was it was still doing its job so why worry, I wondered silently for how long?

Karin's house was nestled in the back of Ginnaton, a Moshov (a state aided village) near the town of Lod. Her dogs barked a lazy greeting, at which a few of the old folk I had come to help with, shuffled forward curiously - my new "family" for the next season. How on earth would I remember all their strange names and understand their babble of Hebrew?

A growing interest in me developed as I washed things and people, learning the odd word that was more frequently used, and needed, as fast as I could. Out of sheer pleasant exhaustion I would fall asleep, despite the rickety bed that my bulging case found use for, it was stuffed underneath the base board and looked suspiciously like and old door, over the broken springs! The bed and lower dollar wage could not deter my spirits as I happily fitted in to this menagre, reminding me of my own home, with similar people staying.

Sunday, my day off, I headed for Jerusalem on a search. To my knowledge there was only one real Christian Book Shop and that was inside the walled city, just through the famous Jaffa Gate. As one walked into the very small shop, the scene before you definitely took you back in time. Books balancing haphazardly in piles, defying gravity and almost daring to be knocked over, while old gospel favourites played from behind the minute glass counter. Benjamen, the owner, that I had befriended on my many visits, ruffled his tufts of grey hair in his hand, it helped him think it seemed. He blinked through his rimless spectacles knowingly as I expressed my need for an evangelical book in Hebrew. He was delighted to help me in my quest, and went off to his storeroom, returning with two books they use for free. One, with a Lion on its cover, held promise, and another, a testimony of a young Hebrew man, equivalent to the Nicky Cruz story (the cross and the switchblade) with a salvation message with answers at the back.

Suddenly, I felt very faint, nausea rising, and collapse seemed imminent.

"Benjamen, can you please pray for me and get me some water?"

The water appeared quicker than the prayer, and I waited expectantly. A not too powerful prayer was agreed upon, and after a while, and having sipped some water, felt I could leave the tiny shop and make my way to the bus that would take me back to Ginnaton, and Karin's safe care.

She took my pulse with her machine and said with alarm, "you're dead!" as nothing had registered. As I felt more dead than alive we laughed in agreement with the machine, but after a sugary cup of tea felt better and remembered to give Karin the books. Delighted tears welled up in her eyes in gratitude. I had noticed that she was a giver and I didn't see many having reciprocated.

That night I was very much alive, prompted by the Holy Spirit, I sat up and chatted with Karin late into the night. My heart sank as I heard her say emphatically, "but I don't believe in God!"

"Lord, how can change her heart and attitude?" I sighed inwardly.

A missionary story dropped into my spirit about a German teacher. As Karin was a German Jew, I knew the story would catch her by surprise! This is the story:

A German teacher was always picking on a young girl in her class, it seemed because she was a Christian and it showed, even in her essays. Jesus got the glory. One day after disciplining the girl unfairly yet again, there was a knock at the classroom door quite loudly. The teacher on opening the door found no one there. To her surprise it happened again, the third time on opening it the teacher dropped down dead by the Holy Spirit! The fear of the Lord came over everyone and the whole village came to know Christ, through a little girl's courage. God will not be mocked, or allow his faithful to be. Vengeance is mine says the Lord!

Karin looked amazed, asked a few questions, then said defiantly, but not convincingly enough, "I still don't believe in God!"

I prayed with her that evening and with the help of the books slowly saw a softening in her spirit.

As my Hebrew had not come on leaps and bounds as Karin had hoped, to enable her to go on a much needed holiday, my time at Ginnaton came to an end. Also, if she had an Israeli helper, she was subsidized in wages due to living on a Moshov.

Another job interview was arranged, and with growing confidence, I caught the bus to Rieshon de Lesion, 45 minutes ride away. I had packed all my things, but left them behind at Karin's. Leaving the main street, I climbed the steep road to the address. The block of flats was built and owned by the Klimker family, I knocked at No.25, and was gratefully greeted by Oren the grandson. A brief interview followed and top dollar wages were settled on, starting immediately. Oren kindly offered to drive me to fetch my luggage, which decidedly needed reviewing. Karin's face was a picture to behold as I arrived in style, and announced that I had come to fetch my things to take to my new job! She had witnessed God answering my prayers. When I have time off and go to visit visit, she proudly invites people to come and meet Mori, my friend that talks to God and He answers her!

***

Pappie Klimker was 94 yrs old, spoke King's English and a couple of European languages. He had been a Managing Director of a large company in Morrocco until he was 88 years old. Mammie Klimker's English was limited, and her jealousy at not being able to follow the conversation between myself and Pappie made life difficult. Her fiery rages at the poor old man were sad to witness.

When he was well enough we would escape downstairs, and out into the sunshine, allowing time to stop and chat to shopkeepers and butchers along the way, jogging his fading memory of happier days long gone. Proudly holding my arm, he would slowly amble back up the stairs to be greeted warmly by Mammie, who had forgot her former anger, she had missed him and wanted to know who we had seen and what was their news?

Mammie had gladly given over the shopping and cooking to me. One day she announced that her sisters Filipina carer was fetching fowls from the Shooken market in Jerusalem for us for supper. On my return from other shopping I found two fowls, still feathered, with their gory throats cut laying on the kitchen table waiting for my attention! My instruction was that I defeathered the carcasses, chopped them into cooking portions, and froze what was not to be used. My determination to show her that I could do the task she thought I could, or would not, tackle, made me succeed. She returned from yet another visit to her sister, who lived in the block as well, whilst I was busy with my chore. I knew she had organized this exercise on purpose when I saw her look of glee. Her face soon changed to open admiration as dinner was on the go and everything else packed neatly away.

"I'm not an African for nothing!" I said tongue in cheek, laughing inwardly at her surprise.

I outdid myself as then she demanded a dinner party, so family and friends could see how well her 'maid' can cook.

One day it was just a bit much! I had to take Pappie to the Doctors... unchartered territory. To make matters worse his regular taxi driver was on holiday, so no English, and it was not one of Pappie's good days, so explanations were haphazard. Mammie had gone to the hairdresser, and in desperation, after running the taxi meter up sky high, I phoned Oren for help. With supper long overdue, I got back four hours later to find Mammie toasting the large Matzov biscuits, with flames rising out the toaster machine. Pulling the plug out the socket was the quickest thing I could think to do and the flames slowly subsiding. I caught a quick glimpse of Mammie's astonished face with singed eyebrows and fringe, and even though it was a serious situation, I laughed until I cried, with Mammie joining me out of sheer relief. The flat was still intact and a new toaster purchased promptly the next day. Mammie was teased by the family about wanting to claim the insurance money for the whole block of flats!

One morning the Lord, woke me up with the words 'Daniel needs you.' I had not seen that young South African man since I left the hostel, which now months ago. Where would I find him? The only thing I could think of was to catch a bus to Tel Aviv, and then another to the hostel.

As I made my way to the 4th floor of the bus terminal again, waiting for the very same bus was Daniel! He was so badly sunburnt and parched, in relief he broke down, with tears welling up in his eyes in gratitude to see me. He had worked so hard in Israel, gone to visit Egypt where he had been robbed and forced to hitchhike back to Tel Aviv and to familiar territory, the hostel. I was able to pay for him at the hostel until he got cash and cards sorted.

I took him for a meal, which he washed down with a few beers. I left him with enough cash till his own money came through, as phoning his family had been priority. It was a privilege to pray with Daniel and give God glory before heading back to my work!

***

My cousin, Lynne, also worked as a carer in the UK. She was encouraging me to come over as I could earn four times my wages and settle my debt to Ev quicker. Her calls were more frequent and I was exhausted from the inconsistent moods of Mammie, with her demands of more chores. And I was so often awakened by Pappie's nocturnal bedwetting, which was not giving me enough rest at all. After much prayer, the song "Arise, shine for your light has come" came to me.

As it was my day off, I decided to catch a bus to see the Dead Sea. Having to leave before sunrise to catch a bus to Jerusalem, where the bus to Eilat left from. Its journey passed, and stopped at, the Engedi Spa, which was where I was heading. The small tourist shop held everything that one needed to soak in the Dead Sea. The salt content that allowed the buoyancy so one could only float on the top of the water, the salt coral on the seafloor was very sharp and cut deep if plastic sandals were not worn as one walked to a depth suitable for the individual. Once again as I noticed a Millennium postcard that had a beautiful sunrise picture with the words *Arise, shine your light has come* printed in gold. It left me no doubt in my mind that I was meant to leave Israel.

Firstly, I would have to extend my visa on my passport by one month, as flights out of the country were full due to celebrating Pessah, (Jewish Easter holiday) which lasted about ten days. To be prepared was always my motto, so I trudged a good five blocks away to the offices of the Minister of Interior. The crowds stood, pushed together hopelessly trying to get through the security gate whilst the poor guard tried to fend off the mob, all wanting visas of some sort. But the door was closed

- lunch break for the people in the office, the only day they stay open for longer than four hours!

Got an idea! Get up before sun up and be first in the queue, well actually fourth, as three others had the same idea. They were well settled, bracing themselves for the crowd that slowly grew in size. Funny, I don't remember how I got in the middle of the mob once again.

Once the gate was opened I had this flash vision of a big hand flattening me to the map of Israel with the words *God's got his hand on you* with me yelling "let me out."

I had noticed that I had lost some weight with all this trailing back and forwards, which was the only consolation as I saw the funny side of this image. After this futile attempt, I had no choice but to wait due to a five week strike for more pay that was now on.

As Pessah ended, I stormed down that Friday to be faced with the stark steel gates locked and no people. My prayers had been answered, so I thought, until a neighbouring shop owner arrived to open his shop, sombrely informed me, "they don't open on Friday's."

"What was the strike for then? They seemed overpaid for the few hours they put in anyway!"

My daily reading did nothing to relieve my annoyance or frustration at my plans being thwarted. It said, 'What you felt unable to cope with can be overcome, moment by moment.' That really got me! Short of growing wings, this is where I was to stay for the next few weeks. I could picture heavenly cherubs brushing up my patience and longsuffering, as I learned to wait for God in his time, as the Visa was vital to me being allowed to return to Israel, in the future.

***

With my extended visa stamped, the rather more than an interested look from the woman behind the desk made me get the feeling that it was time to leave. The only travel agent I had noted was along Ben Yudah Street in Tel Aviv, near the hostel. They boasted brightly coloured inviting adverts on their windows, I soon found that inside was a different story, with a lot of long excuses.

Prompted to go to Jerusalem, I took a wander between the old and new city. A McDonalds' fast food restaurant with loud music drew me in to have a bite of familiar food, I felt this was another sign to leave. Once again outside, in the haze of brilliant sunshine, I wended my way through the maze of little streets. Suddenly I came upon two travel agents tucked away. As all of the agents were busy at the one shop, I quickly ducked into the second and sat before an empty desk. I stared into the face of a petite woman with loud ginger hair, who smiled warmly and greeted me with "Shalom." She was most helpful, and I walked away with a Monarch chartered plane ticket tucked away, having paid considerably less than quoted in Tel Aviv, with only a few days left to fly out.

Oren, disappointed at my finalized decision, organised my replacement from the Agency at last. A sweet Russian woman who, via Oren, had come under pain of death at not meeting up with my expectations and good reputation from the agency. I had three days to teach her all she had to know, leaving her recipes, individual instructions and introducing her to shop owners that could, and would be, helpful. The Russian lady's English was very limited, but Pappie could speak Russian, I could for see another storm cloud brewing over No.25. thanks to the suspicious and jealous mind of Mammie. Oren arrived bearing farewell gifts that I could not have afforded, with a glowing reference.

Karin kindly came to fetch me, as my flight was at 4am and she lived near the airport. She was delighted to have me "sleep" over, and happy to shuttle me to catch my flight. Sleep was not to be had, as it was her first grandchild's christening the next day and food galore needed to be prepared, as was customary. I just got stuck in to help, until the task was complete. I met my replacement, and Karin's new Israeli assistant. This woman was taken aback when, as we prayed before I left the house, I had a prophetic word of knowledge for her. This revealed her stand with God - tears of repentance and fond hugs followed as last goodbyes were said.

Once again, I faced the tirade of interrogation from the militant customs at the airport. My luggage was looking decidedly more respectable, leaving a large portion in Karin's care. I walked proudly through to exchange most of my dollars into British sterling. A stop at the Ladies powder room was necessary first. In true African style I had kept all my notes in my bra. I had not been able to open a Bank account, as foreign workers were illegal, even though it was the done thing all over Israel - I had been told that even the American ambassador had one! The notes had changed my shape for the better, and I called it my XXX (cross your heart bra) Bank, much to everyone's amusement. It was mid-May, the beginning of the scorching summer, and the heat was intense already. The marble tiles used to cool all the homes did little to alleviate the rising temperatures. As I climbed the steps up into the aircraft, with a crown emblem on its tail, I felt this plane had been sent by the King of King's, Jesus, to pick me up, ready to take me to new adventures.

PS: Karin and I have remained wonderful friends since. Four years later, when I was back on a flash visit, she picked me up at the same spot outside the airport. The same car, a little cleaner to honour my visit, (now the age could really show) but faithfully got us back to the Moshov. The home now empty, the old folk long gone. I prayed that they went to glory after introducing them to METV Christian station, encouraging them to sing along to the praise and worship!

We laughed at the memories. Ten pleasant days passed all too quickly between resting and being taken to a Turkish flea market. That was entertaining to say the least, stalls of all sorts, from underwear, to strawberries, to china teapots. Benjamin's shop was a must, to get Karin a Hebrew Bible. She was delighted at the latest gift, along with a pretty nightie. She shyly said she had a Messianic friend now, and was inviting friends to come meet "my friend Mori, who speaks to God!" God had done a work, the difficult times fading, as with hindsight His glory to behold!

I think of the time spent in Israel, with such fondness and gratitude. To have been privileged to partake in a unique experience in a very special nation. I urge anyone to have the guts to visit and evangelise as best we can, Jesus needs YOU to!

Marie, you are the most impressive person that we have met in London! You are like a diamond, clear right through…

EDUARD, LINA AND MINDAGUS

The one person I can rely on is Marie, she does great and wonderful things for as many that will allow her. A real and practical Christian, an amazing prophetess, who speaks straight from the Lord.

She has encouraged me to get back in touch with God, prayed for me, taken me to wonderful churches, and I have been so lucky to have this experience with her. She knows what she wants, and where to look. Inspiring many to change and follow God.

CANDICE DE BRUYN

WHAT R U HATCHING, A GULL OR AN E-GULL (EAGLE)?

Unless you really mean business with God, don't ask Him what He wants you to do, or where he wants you to go, as He WILL take you up on that! You can have what you say!

As a particular live-in care job came to an end, in the beautiful Cotswolds. I asked God where did he want me to go? I heard 'The Island of Jersey.' Was that God or my own desires? I, as a young person, had been besotted with all of Gerald Durrell's books of adventures. Going to foreign lands, with strange customs, to catch animals that could become extinct. To bring them safely back to his Zoo on the island of Jersey; Jersey being one of the group of Channel Islands owned by Britain. Princess Anne, being the patron of the Zoo, swells the interest of the visitors and islanders alike with her visits. It had been a dream of mine to visit this now world famous Zoo. To see these rare species, long read about over and over, many times laughing aloud at the compromising situations the team found themselves in. Once all the books were read, I found that *Beasts in my Bed* written by Jackie Durrell, Gearld's wife, from a woman's point of view, was just as funny, due to the things she had to put up with!

Interestingly, a job on Jersey had come up, and I had gone for and interview. I was not chosen, disappointed, I found myself another and travelled to the Cotswolds with a heavy heart. This task was also not an easy one and as it came to an end, I had an urgent phone call from Pam, the daughter from the Jersey job! Their first choice having failed them, they wanted me as soon as possible to look after George, their father, on Jersey. I caught the bus from the Cotswolds down to Oxford, and was met by Pam, driven smartly south to Southampton to catch a light plane over. As the plane struggled against the wind it made groaning noises, with my imagination running, I could picture it coming apart like watching a comic strip, but prayer came easily to my lips.

On landing, I walked carefree at Pam's side through the airport, and jumped into a black cab. This was not London, it seemed strange but I was also glad to have something familiar to relate to. We soon arrived at Les Sablons, George's home, which was nestled behind the famous Royal Jersey Golf Club and Course. There were many French names of places, homes and roads on this small island as it was only a few miles off the French coast. If you screwed up your eyes against the glare on a good day, the buildings along the French coast could be vaguely seen.

George had been a semi-pro golfer in his time, with trophies, dotted around the home, but he now had to be satisfied with watching (or making suggestions to any that would listen). The long balmy summer days stretching late in the evening, allowed me to push George, in his wheelchair, to enjoy watching a late golfer teeing off, or just to sit and take in the long view of Gorey beach. The gulls circling around above our heads, hoping we had some tit bits. Their cries fading on the breeze as they wavered in the air, before swooping to grab whatever their sharp eyes had spotted. The fat baby gulls often looked larger than the parent birds, they even looked lost as they stomped aimlessly about.

With a mixture of good natured stubbornness, and a gleeful sense of humour, George and I got on famously!

My cousin Lynne had just arrived back from South Africa and had two weeks to wait for her job to begin on the UK mainland. George kindly allowed her to come and stay for the time. Playing tour guide on my off time, allowed me to see other parts of the island I had not yet seen. Another visit to the Zoo, a must. As Lynne and I drove through the windy, narrow lanes we had a giggle at the brave seagulls, who had flown inland to the island's farms, pecking away freely in the fields, holding no fear for the scarecrows that were to frighten them off. The Honesty Box, with its slits to place your money in for your choice of produce purchased, was an interesting concept which could challenge one's conscience! This would NOT work back in South Africa where people seem to think it was right to help themselves to anything, and everything, at will.

Being close to the Halloween season, Lynne and I, despite our disbelief of the occasion, had to laugh at the spectacle, this one farm in particular had put on show. Grim and grinning faces cut out of pumpkins of all sizes, leered at us as we suddenly rounded a corner and came upon this pumpkin family. The barn was decorated with silhouettes of black cats and a witch, looking as if she had just landed, or about to take off! One could appreciate the artistic effort at any rate. Taking a break from our sightseeing, we stopped at a delightful tea room with roses and dainty climbing flowers which spilled over the stone walls, enclosing the tables set in the sunshine. Fat homemade scones, butter, strawberry jam, with thick Jersey cream were a must. Tea in flowery bone china, tasted good after driving around.

At last it was time for my dear cousin to start her awaited job. I was sad to see her leave, and waved goodbye, praying that she had been sufficiently refreshed to handle her next assignment. Lynne had not been well, with bladder cancer for some time, and bravely, got on with tasks at hand. Fond memories of her visit to cherish!

St.Helier was the capital town on the island. I had to drive in once a week for some specialities from Marks and Spencer, and from George's favourite shop at the open market, which he had supported for years, as they had the best of seafood. The many stalls and shops held favourite delights to take home to enjoy. The market boasted of a small Christian book room, the only one I knew. One of the workers, a pastor's wife, knew of a UK gospel singer I had been privileged to hear thirty years ago in South Africa, and I still sing one of the songs she sang then. George had various people working for him - Helen, a petite light redhead, did any odd job possible. She answered an advert for an 'odd job man'. There were others who performed tasks in, and around, the property during the week. Helen and I got on famously! Our love of Jesus and wacky senses of humour were our common denominator. I was cheerfully invited to her church, the Anglican, about a mile up the road from Les Sablons. The church was the one George's family had attended over the years, for social events and more recently the funeral of his late wife. The family expressed to me that they were not impressed with the lack of visitation by the Rector, who had not been too shy to ask for a considerable sum of money for a new organ for the church, and not visited since! Now I had two good reasons to meet the erring Rector, to pull his ear and get George a visit, while boosting Helen's favour, having me add to the lean numbers attending service. They all looked pretty starchy to me, hats not being my scene, and so did nothing to impress or intimidate me either! As Jersey was a tax haven for mostly millionaires, fine feathers make fine birds or do they? A few weeks with bunch, and I could tell they all sounded as they looked, they were on the road to nowhere and were happy to go there! That did not suit me at all. Helen and her varied lifestyle was more to my liking.

I heard that Terry Law, an evangelist of note, was coming to speak at the Elim Church, in the centre of St. Helier. He was a speaker who was not to be missed. I had heard him the previous year in London, and was enthralled with his testimonies of adventures around the world, so an interesting evening promised.

The most memorable stories were told, not to be forgotten. An old Eskimo man who was crying after receiving Salvation, challenged Terry at not coming sooner, as his wife had recently died, and without salvation. This story should make us quicker to talk openly about our faith, and be able to challenge people on their eternal destiny. NO FEAR OF MAN'S OPINION NEEDED, ONLY GOD'S, when he asks us why we did not tell the people.

"My people perish through lack of knowledge."

Having ordered the tape of Terry's talk for Helen to enjoy, it was necessary to return on the Sunday. I reasoned, I may as well go to the morning service. While waiting for Sunday, I had a vision of two people upside down, head first in the sand up to their waist, what was this Lord? The first thing that came to mind, was that the two people did not want to face, or tackle, a situation, instead pretending it was not happening! During the service I had a vision. I spoke it out; I saw a watchman on a wall, blowing a trumpet, and as he started to blow the wall started to crumble, and I felt that God wanted the walls that had been built within the church to be broken down, and now was the time to start! At the end of the service a lady with a Spanish accent came and flung her arms around me, saying, "thank goodness you've come, where are you from, how long can you stay?"

I said, laughing, "God brought me, and it is up to God how long I'm here."

She introduced herself as Maria, yet another Maria - my relief carer's name was Maria. She invited me for coffee on my off time, the next day and a friendship started.

Another lady with a husky soft voice said "How did you get here?"

"By car I just live in Grouville!"

"I meant, how did you get on to the island?"

"Flew in an aeroplane!" I suggested, tongue in cheek, mischievously.

My sense that I was not quite getting the picture added to my amusement, and Sue's frustration no end.

"We can't talk now, but we need to meet!"

Phone numbers exchanged with a promise to explain her riddle type questions! How naïve I was then, which was just as well, as I may not have been so willing to obey by being there after all, but there was a task at hand. I could feel it in my spirit, feeling almost pregnant with expectation. It was the pastor's turn to investigate my potential, as I most definitely was feeling to make Elim my spiritual home. He was a lovely man, with a sound teaching ministry, open to any suggestions to edify the church. His wife played piano and organ well. Having sung and lead worship I was soon drawn into the music team, helping lead, sing solos and give small teachings as I got prophetic revelation. The music team grew with enthusiasm as understanding of worship grew, and how important their role actually was! With God's guidance, I was able to make a definite shift in the spirit, with much prayer backing from my intercessors, back home in South Africa and locally.

Fasting was needed, as WAR had been declared on the Jezebel spirit entrenched in the church! Breakthrough had to be close as the attack came! From the sheet music, to the song sheets, to overheads disappearing to disrupt the flow, to underlying factors, such as people of long standing in the church demanding their favourite seats, control in leadership, traditions given place, to the pianist's fear of the anointing! I encouraged a team to get together, to do street evangelism on a Friday night, to draw the teenagers off the streets, curbing drinking and anti-social behaviour, which kicked off a meeting with a difference. Flyers were also distributed as invitations and I couldn't resist chucking a bunch into the Freemason's Temple postbox. A large, silent building along the same road, up from our church. I was told that many businesses and key governmental positions were held by Freemasons on the island. Also, that a certain beach on the North of the island, with steep cliffs, was known as the Devil's Hole, where Satanists held blood sacrifices. All this added to the spiritual, and oppressive, control over the island. Sue had warned me about on arrival. Freemasons and Satanists are one in the same. The only thing with Freemasons, is that only the few at the top of the ranks, know that they are leading innocent men, (and in USA, women too) to worship the Devil and eternal destiny, therefore Hell. Satanist, don't even disguise that fact! This all contributed to the general believers being lukewarm, not understanding the full impact of the implications of the oppression. It is interesting, that now, five years later, there has been an investigation into children disappearing, and body parts have discovered at a children's home on the Island of Jersey! Proving the point!

The island is only five miles by nine miles in size, and holds many stories behind the colourful Jersey stone walls, not unlike the colour of the stone used in Israel to build. George generously got extra help in as I got more involved at Elim, enjoying me regaling him of different incidents through my eyes! As I was in charge overall, there was another war on the go when I found food disappearing, and the culprit reprimanded! Other than that incident the days passed pleasantly, making George's life as fulfilling as possible. His children shuttled back and forth, visiting in turns, which added interest, as did the gardeners' weekly visit, to which George contributed his ideas. We awaited the new blooms opening, a peek of the haze of colour gradually developing, as we checked daily on their progress.

As time went on, I had a vision of me as a midwife, helping turn a baby in the womb, so it could be birthed. The baby appeared, it was a bird, looking like a baby gull. As the vision continued, I saw the bird plod its way along the road, past Helen's Anglican Church. This revelation was interesting, as if the new thing birthed had not been invited to stop there and was looking for a place to feel welcomed, just like the Holy Spirit looks for a welcome home within us!

The next week the vision I was shown was cracked, dry brittle ground. Slowly big spots of water started to plop on the dry ground, to becoming rain! Suddenly there was grass growing up. My goodness, the vision continued even as I walked to church that morning from the car park. By the time I took the platform for the morning service, the grass was almost waist high. I saw a hand with a sickle raised to harvest the long grass. The song "It's Beginning To Rain" sprung to mind and I quickly taught the music team and congregation. As it sunk deep into their spirits, the power of God fell, and as we sang it over and over, allowing the anointing to wash over us! Some people fell back into their seats under the power. An awesome presence filled the place as people came to grips with the Almighty God! The drought had broken! Ground reclaimed from the enemy, as understanding and rejoicing followed! "You're a seer!" exclaimed Tony, after a long quietness had overcome him.

"Yes, I am prophetic," I agreed, at the almost accusation!

On the medical side, George was deteriorating quickly. At almost 92 years old, what did we expect? Even though I had done a reassuring job of salvation with him, I felt the errant Rector needed to be called. (With George, being of the old school.) Knocking on the Rector's manse door, I demanded his company for tea that same day, with the urgency in mind, which was not what he was used to. (He had not met anyone like me yet, who determinedly got the job done, to whoever's inconvenience!)

Later that afternoon, setting up a trolley, of tea with dainty cakes and salmon and cucumber sandwiches for George and his visitor, I was annoyed no end to hear talk of golf rather than heaven. The Rector thought the visit went rather well, until George died. The man had the grace to relay the story against himself, realizing that George's sense of humour had caught him out! He had asked George why had he built his house so near to the golf course, did he like golf?

"Hate the stuff," said the ex-pro golfer with tongue in cheek!

The blushing Rector only found out he had been had when the family helped him make the obituary speech for the funeral. George had the last laugh! With George's poor appetite, my culinary skills had not been made full use of. Pam was suitably impressed, with the food I had provided for the wake, which was praise indeed, as she owned a restaurant on mainland UK! George had died, I had birthed the spiritual baby, or so I thought, feeling my task on Jersey was finished, I so started to plan my departure back to South Africa.

***

"Would a mother leave her chick for the ravens to kill?" God's voice angrily, challenged me early one morning! I saw four black ravens pecking a baby bird to death and I knew I could not leave. At the same time the family asked me to stay with full pay until the assessors had been out from London to view the property - they took their time about coming over, exactly a month!

God knew I hadn't finished the spiritual job, so He used my bankcard next to keep me where He wanted me. My card's expiry date was due, and a new one ordered from mainland. I have since learnt that timing and waiting on God is so important, trying to hurry the process only frustrates oneself. (And maybe God too!)

The vision I had originally was of two people with their heads stuck in sand, ignoring all the things that needed changing, in fear of offending man and not enough fear of God. I believe it was the dear pastor and his wife. So after the breakthrough, it was announced they were moving, to pastor another church on a neighbouring island! I had mixed feelings, a dear friend was leaving, but I was excited to find out what God was up to, finding a suitable divine replacement at this crucial spiritual time was a daunting task!

The month ending, I now had to move out of Les Sablons. Noella, kindly had me stay in her flat, as she knew I felt God had not finished using me on the island, or church. Her obedience will be rewarded.

It was decided to hold a farewell dinner mainly organised by Noella, with songs of celebration, sketches, and ticket draws for prizes for the lucky ticket holders. I had collected the prizes from businesses, who donated gifts from haircuts to cinema tickets, DVDs, sweets, perfume etc. The evening was a success and enjoyed by all. The final church farewell service was well attended, I celebrated with many associates across the board, who immensely enjoyed the short sketch I wrote. It highlighted many incidents that were very funny, maybe rather forgotten, but worth a last laugh! I had chosen the 'actors' carefully and the whole thing went off rather well. The audience laughed in delight, not only at the humour, but at the bravado to put it on.

Thanks were said to one and all, farewells were said, and a feast, put a close to the evening.

An Indian evangelist, John, came to hold a crusade. A Jamaican lady, that Lynne had befriended whilst on the island, and whom I had invited to this meeting, started manifesting demons! Pat was a lady I soon got acquainted with, I could see she knew, like myself, what to do. We got the woman to the ladies' powder room and set her free, while the more average illnesses were being dealt with at the altar. Pat, a missionary, evangelist teacher at heart, had been out to Kenya teaching yearly, or as her health permitted. What an evening of rejoicing! Pat and I have remained firm friends since.

Now we were waiting to interview of a possible pastor, one of a few in line to interview was trying, and much prayer agreed upon! One Saturday morning, awakening in the Spirit, the heaviness of the Lord held me down, I could not even turn over in bed!

'The one that's coming, you're not fit to tie his shoes,' the Lord's voice said strongly. "I know, I'm not fit to tie YOUR shoes Lord!" was my humble answer. "YOU DON'T UNDERSTAND!" HE proclaimed, "THE ONE THAT'S COMING TODAY!" I could hear the frustration in His voice. Then I understood!

There was a pastor coming over from mainland that day and I was to tell the elders that HE was the man for the job! Interestingly, I had now also had a revelation, which identified the four ravens in my previous vision! I phoned a lady deacon, with whom I related well, and told her of my experience. She promised to pass the information on, as the pastor to be interviewed, and his wife, were actually staying with her family. Due to the famous fog that often clouded the island, trapping people unawares, they would not be leaving the island and would be at the morning service anyway! God is so good! God had shown me that he had prepared Stephen's heart to apply, and that he was well aware of any hiccups that still needed ironing out!

Stephen took the morning service, and the meeting did not go as people expected, as Stephen's prophetic authority was soon challenging and putting things in order! I sat praying as the church was in the final stages of being put the right way up!

"Yes, Lord, get them!"

Stephen asked for the lady who sang with the mike. That was strange, as there were four of us that sang with mikes. As I was sitting farther back for space, I watched each of the other women in the music team get up in turn, Stephen saying "No, it's not you," until he came to me. I could imagine how David must have felt in the field alone, finding out he was the one to be anointed! I was given an amazing word and tears fell as what I had birthed in secret was now being shown publicly! He then called upon his wife, God had shown her that the congregation now were all baby Eagles! I could not stop crying in joy, understanding my bird birth in full now! Stephen got the position and I sensed I could leave my 'babies' in good hands.

***

Sue had explained that even telephone lines were tapped if they knew you were a strong Christian, so it was not surprising for me to be intercepted by immigration when my six month visa was outstayed, let alone the fact that I was working without a work visa. God allowed them to release me as I was leaving the country anyway! These finances earned were to do a big task back home in South Africa. The exchange rate rose sharply to my favour, to God be the Glory, as another assignment was satisfactorily completed!

P.S - I had the desire to return to Jersey years later to the see first-hand the fruit of the past adventure. Due to my visa history problems I had been wary of returning before I go release from the Lord. When I was in Ireland my precious friend Carolla suggested I go to visit Jersey, as a friend Paul was on the ship Logos Hope, an Operation Mobilization library ship that travelled the world making the bible and related material cheaply available.

After much vacillating, I believed that the Lord wanted me to leave Belfast on this venture. After leaving Belfast, I passed through Dublin, touching base with Fiona whom God had used me to help there, and continued to London. Having not much cash for breakfast, or anything else other than travel, I made my way to the Victoria Station area to kill the few hours before my bus to Bournemouth, where the ferry (which Pat on Jersey had kindly paid for) would take me to Jersey.

Feeling hungry, I popped into a cafe. It had an open bay window, artistically framing two ladies sitting inside, dressed smartly with hats on sitting inside, which drew me inside. I commented to the ladies on how lovely they looked against the window, which started an interesting conversation - one lady was meeting HRH Prince Charles for lunch, and the other Al Gore for dinner!

I had felt the Holy Spirit say, 'You can chose any breakfast you like.' Me being conservative, chose a cheaper breakfast, not the one I would have preferred. Having shared my excitement of my journey, they, with polite interest listened, and as they made a move to leave, one gently laid £10 on my table said, "Your breakfast is also paid for, God Bless, you're in our prayers."

That £10 was going to pay for my night in Bournemouth, another miracle. God led me to the ferry leaving time was at the crack of dawn the following day!

The Lord had shown me a blanket of white cloud of anointing prayer, from the ships' staff, over the island, and that I was to come in under that Cover. It was to be my protection from the run in with immigration from the last visit, and felt like the spies that Rahab sheltered. Pat, my dear, obedient friend, joyfully met me and arrangements to meet Paul the next day were organized.

Paul's host family kindly picked me up in their smart car and took us out for a bite to eat and then asked, where we like to go to have time to relax and chat, to catch up with our mutual friends. Without hesitation I said Gorey Pier, usually a hive of activity and interest. I did notice a quick smile flash across Paul's face but let it go.

On arriving he chuckled and explained that there were small teams from the Christian boat on assignment, that they had no money, place to stay, or food and they had to see how God would provide for them. This was their third day. As Paul and I walked down the festive pier the young folk were spotted. Paul and I agreed to take them to lunch, he with the young man and me with the two girls. Their faces were a picture as they lit up at this surprise treat. I was able to minister to the young ladies, who confided how down they really were, and ready to give up on God, missions and pretty much everything. Lessons in faith were learnt fast as God gently challenged, loved, guided them, through my testaments of how I had got through challenges with faith, trust and obedience ... Amy was steaming mad with God and the situation! God told me to tell her to stop being so angry with him, and they had really asked God for chocolate, so dug deep and handed £5 note to Pabalo saying, "and God says this is for chocolate!" They both were so gobsmacked and encouraged to carry on and never, give up! We prayed for God's provision as nightfall was drawing near. Our time at Gorey was over.

On arriving to visit the ship the next day, I heard from the girls about God's provision since I had left them, there was ecstatic chatter, introductions all round and soon stories were shared to encourage a group around a dining table. One young man in the group, called Justin, also stuck in my mind. My visit to my Elim church was disappointing, but necessary, and then there was the long return journey back to Belfast via London. My husband Alex phoned me to say he had put £300 in my bank account, which was one of the highlights of my day. Reaching London Victoria, again I felt impressed to go to use the Ladies cloakroom at the Thistle Hotel. There I started a conversation with a lady who took great interest in my unusual vocation. Shegave me her business card, and invited me to come and speak at a do the following week in London. Wow, Mitty was the UK President for Women and for World Peace!

The devil tried to stop me by landing me in hospital in Belfast with agonizing gallstones for a week! I soon felt much better, convinced that my fast recuperation was due to my darling husband Alex flying over to be with me, and the power of agreement with him in prayer. I persuaded the doctors, that I was indeed commissioned to speak, and they reluctantly discharged me out the hospital.

The evening in Lancaster Gate was a grand success, with me receiving a certificate of recognition, an Ambassador of Peace Award, for my contribution toward World Peace acknowledging my work as a missionary to bring peace, women's empowerment and rights! God is faithful, what you do in secret will be rewarded openly.

P.P.S - Two years later, I was still stuck in London, at God's pleasure! Having had to go through so much, been beaten near to death and homeless on the streets, I was thankful for God's divine provision in accommodation etc. Now, through a string of divine contacts I went to a South African church one Sunday morning, knowing God said that is where I should worship that morning. I looked around the auditorium for a few young folk that God had used me with, and hoped to see in the service. I saw a girl stare at me with amazement. She looked familiar, but also looked like another friend Marilyn, who was also a double for a dear friend Louise in South Africa. As my memory sped through all these possibilities, the girl said, "it's Amy, from the boat on Jersey." It was Amy and Justin from the Logos Hope Ship on Jersey, two years ago. We exchanged warm greetings and lunch following the church service, to catch up! Amy had lost my email address and had been asking God to let her meet me again. Justin was also excited and told me how I had encouraged him when I chatted round the table that day on the boat. Now they were both were going through challenges, in London, as only London can dish out, and God sent me to encourage them once again. These young people have not given up. Amy is now in charge of organizing 'line up' for the ship, to come into port in United Kingdom in June. Excitement filled my spirit as Amy asked if I would speak to encourage when the ship came to port. I delightedly accepted and saw God open doors again that no man could open. I naturally didn't foresee, but as the Lord changes things for His Glory, I relax and go with the quick flow of the river of the Holy Spirit. I too grow daily in Grace, as I see God extend more grace to me daily, giving me time to make up on things I have not had the time to, with all the pressures I have had to contend with and pray through!

Praise God!!

Marie Parnes is a strong woman of God. She knows, and loves, the Word of God and applies the Word to every area of her life. Marie teaches biblical principles with strong prophetic leanings. She has been a blessing to our ministry and I recommend readers to truly grasp what God wants to impart through her.

MARTIN TRUSLER
PASTOR OF MIGHTY RIVER MINISTRIES
MARGATE, SOUTH AFRICA

SOUTH AFRICA - WE WALK BY FAITH

As the South African sun scorched down onto our uncovered flesh, turning it rosy pink, I grimaced at the discomfort. As a South African, I had been through this many times before, and by nightfall I knew we would, , be a brilliant red, skin taught and very painful. Mentally working out our limited finances, I decided that catching any taxi would be considered a luxury, but necessary with our luggage, that my dearly beloved was once again, loudly complaining at to having to help carry around. African taxi ranks are a hive of noisy chatter, in various volumes of determined excitement, as convincing conversations progressed. Sellers with almost overripe fruit, luke-warm cans of cool drinks and cheap and wrapped sweets, now sticky from the sun, as it uncooperatively slowly moved, making the protective shade of the bright umbrellas, disappear, that were desperately needed. The smell of cooking food, with hope for selling at a profit, turned my stomach with the thought of health and hygiene, the flies shooed casually away, to return immediately, while the sun turned the 'feasts' it into a food poison zone. Oh well, they all look overweight, what doesn't kill, fattens, obviously.

Having been directed to an energetically, washed red TOYOTA HI- ACE, with 16 seats fitted, we apologised for our luggage, that had to take up a seat. It was no problem, we would just have to pay a passenger fare for a seat for the extra luggage that could not squash onto our laps. We were tightly crammed in, and the smell of human odour was rising to nauseas proportions in the heat.

Finally, we lurched into action after a considerable wait, as the taxi, could not leave, until it was full of passengers! (A rule we found ran nation-wide!) Never mind, if one needed to get somewhere in a hurry this was the well-known 'African time' excuse.

Togetherness, the reassuring driver, with his large white teeth, gleaming (looking like an advert for Colgate toothpaste) in his dark shiny face, (I wonder how 'together' he really is), as he weaves his TOYOTA High Impact Culling Equipment, Hi-Ace for short, through the rush hour traffic. Occasionally, using the pavement to increase productivity. The sun shines brightly off Togetherness' gleaming, stolen BMW hubcaps. Togetherness is a confident man with high spirits, as evidenced by the stickers on his rear window: GOD LOVES TAXI DRIVERS and AVOID CONSTIPATION – TRAVEL BY TAXI.

On the front of his taxi, between a large dent, which, ominously, was in the shape of a large traffic cop, and the holes from a small spray of bullets, is a lurid notice reading: JUKSKEI PARK EXPRESS INAUGURAL FLIGHT – the word "flight" is Togetherness' personal joke. What we are witnessing is the inaugural leg of what is hopefully to become a daily service between Jukskei Park and Johannesburg – a 25 km journey which takes 10 minutes – less if the pavements are open. The percussion waves from Togetherness' powerful radio (taken from a BMW Z3), pushes back the mirage of the heat on the road. He is playing Boom Shakas's latest hit on low frequency, 120 DB. (How low can we go?). In my bank years, seven stories up, the loudness of the music of these taxis, made the windows of our offices rattle, as they took their place waiting at the traffic lights, revving their engines, in preparation to get ahead. Togetherness hoots as he drives. Taxi drivers often hoot to passers-by they know, Togetherness hoots at anything he sees including trees – as is his custom.

On board the taxi are now ALL white people. They do not come any whiter than this – they are OMO (A South African, washing powder) white. They were not born white, no their pallor is due to fear and stark terror. Take John, never in his life has he done 0 to 100 km/h in six seconds - especially not in heavy traffic. He is gripping the seat in front of him so tightly, that he notices his fingertips have gone transparent, as a passing taxi fires a brief burst from an automatic-weapon in his direction. Denise's colour has changed from green-black to a sort of waxen ivory as quickly as the last traffic light had changed to red (a colour which traditionally prompts taxi drivers to make more haste).

Togetherness regularly looks over his shoulder while driving – even for a full minute – asking passengers their destinations. Elizabeth, sitting right at the back, has opportunity to say "Rendbeg Senta," even though she works in Jennesburg. Randburg was coming up fast and it suddenly seemed near enough for her, at only 20kms to walk. She worries about how she will make her way to the front – but only fleetingly, because the taxi has now reached Randburg Centre and Togetherness has stopped. He has stopped as suddenly as a plane might stop up against a mountain. Now EVERYBODY is at the front in a warm, intimate heap. Elizabeth alights as gracefully as anybody can with one knee locked behind the other. She is vaguely aware of passers-by loosening her clothing and shouting "give her air!"

Togetherness bowls happily along Jan Smuts Avenue, overtaking a police BMW that is chasing a getaway car. Then he overtakes the getaway car too, exchanging boisterous greetings with the driver, whom he knows. To the concern to all of us still in the taxi, Togetherness is steering with his elbows, because he needs his hands free to check the morning's takings, and to wave to girls on the pavement. What is even more remarkable is that Togetherness is doing this despite the fact that his taxi does not have a steering wheel! When his friend, Sipho, stole this vehicle it was fitted with a steering lock, so Sipho had to remove the steering wheel. The spanner that Sipho has attached to the steering bolt in its place is quite adequate though.

Togetherness smiles and turns to his passengers as he accelerates past a truck on a blind rise. He announces, "Ladies and Gentleman, these ees your

Keptin speeken. We will shortly be lending in Jennesbeg. Plis make sure your seatbelts are in an upright position, end your seats are fastened. Thank you for flying with us today. We hope to see you soon again. Local time is 12 o'clock GMT and 12'ish FAST. (Flexible African Time)" We all unfold as gratefully, and gracefully, as is possible after of the experience of African public transport.

The old saying is that mad dogs and Englishmen go out in the noonday sun. My husband being English, did not appreciate my sense of humour when I mentioning this quote, but agreed that I was most definitely mad to have dragged him halfway around the world for this!

"And this is serving Jesus?" he exploded

"Oh well, you can please some of the people some of the time, but not all the people all of the time!" I quipped, disgruntled myself at the inconvenience of not having a car anymore!

My faithful little four door, white Volkswagen Golf, had been sold for tickets to return to UK, so I could work to restore my bank balance as money ran dry. Never mind that when I had money, I had kindly lent sums of cash to 'friends' whose promises of repayment still have not materialized years later, which could have avoided losing the car! With the climate very different in the South African jobmarket than some years ago, there was no chance of finding work. So a walk by faith was the way forward. Having worked sporadically in the UK, and return airfares paid for, we had landed to continue with our 'mission work' with limited funds. In a Shopping mall in Randburg, near the cheapest place to stay, we bumped into an African pastor, we knew, who had visited Durban with mutual African pastors and friends there. He kindly gave us a 50 Rand note and allowed us the use of his cell phone, to refresh Quintens' convenient memory loss of the substantial amount he owed me still from nearly 18 months ago. Quinten, having established the current urgency of our predicament, banked 1000 Rand in my account - only another 4800 Rand for me to retrieve, and he would be free from the debt! At least the amount returned would pay for us to get the bus from Johannesburg, on our way down south, to Durban and on to the Eastern Cape, there were many hours of travelling ahead. As the familiar terrain of Mt. Ayliff came in view, our spirits rose with excitement as we were welcomed by Pastor Saul and driven proudly, and joyously, back to Mama Sago's family house. Mama's family were quite prominent in the small town, owning a large supermarket, and the Hall in the centre of the village, which was used for visiting preachers Crusades and Pastor Saul's Church meetings. There were hugs and handshakes all round, and after freshening up, we sat down to enjoy a meal, listening to all the latest news.

I had felt that this little country village was to become a spiritual capital in the Eastern Cape, and on sharing this thought with Pastor Saul he confirmed that the Lord had also revealed that to him. We had been asked to speak at a three-day conference which had been organized. Many were touched, refreshed and healed as God visited His people. The tears of thanks were very humbling for

Alex, as always he had complained at great lengths about what we had had to go through to get here. At one of the lunch breaks, Alex spoke into another pastor's life, which secured us future invitations further south. Firstly, to speak at Butterworth. Then even further south, to help at a tent crusade in a very rural area, 32 miles away from Idutwa, the nearest town. Then to be shared with three pastors in different areas of the second biggest African township in South Africa. Makatanze township, on the outskirts of East London, a coastal town, even further south, on the east coast of South Africa. Masiza, pastored two churches in East London, and was the Inspector of Schools for the Eastern Cape, a big man in stature, and importance in the community.

The hall recommended for use in Butterworth was challenging, being out of the town, so transport was difficult in the evening and attendance wasn't the best. Alex's issues in behaviour, double mindedness, and even outbursts of violent anger, escalated as he ignorantly, or wilfully, befriended people that contributed harm to us, in marriage and ministry. As a prophet, I've never been a people pleaser, but have aimed to correct through teaching and example. Here I was walking on a seesaw of eggshells, never quite knowing which way the day would flow, flow being the operative word! The word witchcraft came to me (the word of God says stubbornness is as rebellion is as witchcraft) and with three pastors and myself praying with him to help set him free, we unfortunately didn't have much success at that point. Not because of anything other than the fact that we were praying amiss, and deeper understanding was needed of roots Rejection, Vagabond, Orion and Orphan, and Heredity Spirits abound. His tantrums and demands to leave THEN made it impossible to stay, so we left the rest of the team to minister and went back to Durban for respite!

My friends Andrew and Louise had kindly given us the bus money for return tickets to East London. Having to stop at Idutwa, made the matter worse. As we were to do a week's first steps course, for the new converts from the tent crusade that was ending the day we arrived. So Alex, disappointed and now bored, knew that he was not going to be the man of the hour and soon got the children singing, dancing and following him around like the Pied Piper, which gave them and him hours of fun! He disappeared with them to come back to our host home in the dark of night, jubilant at being used to heal a girl from her sick bed. With no electricity, no running water let alone hot water, no shower, no flush toilet, (just a drop toilet, a hole in the ground some yards away from the house) this was not Alex's cup of tea. Luckily my camping days with my family held me in good stead. Posh hotels, restaurants and homes were more his style! So two days later Alex caused a row with me, packed his things, demanded half the cash for our next leg of our journey, and hitched back to Idutwa, where he could catch a bus back to Durban and the comfort of a 'friend' of mine, and her fine house with pool.

As I do my best to complete any task set before me, I stayed. That evening I called a prayer meeting and was blessed when one of the young women got filled with the Holy Spirit, and began speaking in other tongues. Triumphantly, I did a quick teaching with someone interpreting into the local dialect. The next day, the local pastor and 'crew' came to dismantle the tent. I stood helplessly watching, saddened at Alex's departure. Wandering down the short walk, to the minute shop hoping to purchase air-time for my phone. There were about ten African men sitting along the edge of the road, , drinking beer and other mixes, and smoking – there was a hint of marijuana in the air. I was of obvious interest, which I tried to nonchalantly ignore! I stepped into the earthy smell of the shop, surprised by the darkness, forgetting for a moment that there wasn't any lights. I was warmly greeted by a lady, behind the high wooden counter, who had come to the prayer meeting. My little knowledge of snatches of the language did me sufficiently to wave away the grateful thanks, for being there. Back out in the quickly fading daylight, I was challenged by one of the row of men still sitting, just watching.

"Where's your husband?" a voice out the gloom spoke.

Taken aback, by this unexpected question, I put my guard up to the possible danger I, as a white woman on her own, was in.

As calmly as I could muster, praying popcorn prayers for wisdom, and safety, I said confidently, "He's had to go somewhere, but I'm sure will be back soon."

Please LORD JESUS, send him back, and quickly! Father, you said we were to be a protection for each other, and this word had been confirmed. Jesus be my protection. Now what? Suddenly I had a word of knowledge for a large man who held a stick. This man spoke good English and God revealed to me that he had been brought up by his mother as a Christian and was now for many years backslidden. He was to be a Moses and lead the people to Christ, and that the stick was to represent a staff of correction. I challenged the company of men through this man's interpretation for me at their wrong doings. Tears fell, as one by one removed their hats and knelt before me to come to Christ. As the last man went back to sit down, different!

I ran through the field to fetch the pastor to come and take their names, as the last of the tent was being folded to pack away in the house I slept in. He was smiling from ear to ear. Ten new members for his church!

That night the house prayer meeting was a celebration! The mother, at the end of the meeting, confided that the daughter had been filled with the spirit, and had kept waking her up, seeing things. They shared a room and she wanted to know could I please have her daughter share mine, as the mother had a long days work at a school ahead of her and needed her sleep. I said that was fine, as now I had company other than the candle I kept lit. In the early hours some men somehow got into the house, and the two of us prayed silently for safety. We could hear them sitting on the folded tent and talking, eating food they found leftover in the kitchen, and then eventually leaving. I couldn't sleep, the girl did, waking only with a visitation of the Lord or angels, her eyes as big as saucers in amazement and fear. Through my interpreter the next morning, I was able to explain and understanding and glory replaced fear.

Masiza phoned to say he felt God telling me to leave the location, and thanked me for the work I was able to achieve. I had woken up that morning with that word as well. So hurriedly packed, and a lift into the tiny village was organized. I had reluctantly sold my laptop, that was to be used to write this very book on, due to lack of cash, to a member of the Sago family who still had to give me part payment of a few hundred Rand. After praying, I felt myself led to phone Pastor Saul. He was in Idutwa town itself at a seminar, and could meet me in the break, lend me the money and then get it back from the other man when he returned to Mt.Ayliff! God's faithfulness continued as I noticed a smart shiny new black car starting up and quickly asked which direction they were going... through to Idutwa, 32 miles away, and of course they could give me a lift! The man was a wealthy local shop owner who was trying to persuade Alex and I to come live in the area and start a Christian school, he would provide a house, salary and car, and build the school. The needs are great in this vast terrain. Meeting Pastor Saul so divinely, was awesome. Soon, I was on my way back to join Alex, to try and get him ready for East London.

We bussed down once again, and were met by Masiza and the Pastor we were going to stay with Pastor Lucas and Mama welcomed us warmly. We agreeably worked with Mama at some of the 150 schools in the location, holding the religious platform in the school assemblies, and speaking at a prize giving at a high school. Some of these schools have only six toilets for about 400+ pupils. Once again, the practical needs are great. Alex enjoyed, and performed well in, this environment. We started a small crusade in the classroom of a local school that was made available. I could visualise a huge sports hall one day being built in the centre of the location, that could keep the young people out of mischief during the day whilst doubling as a Church gathering place in the evenings. We saw God perform quite a few miracles, such as the healing of a lady with aids, the hearing of a deaf person was restored, and other more minor healings.

Then an African evangelist from Johannesburg came with fancy everything, as well as a mountain of pride and arrogance! He took over the platform, and intimidated Alex, who once again caused a row with me, and drummed up sympathy from this man. I challenged this man telling him that God had shown me that he was a Goliath. You could see that did not make him happy, and me not liked. This man then demanded any cash from Pastor Lucas and Mama that they could muster for petrol to go to back to Durban, a 20 hour journey away. I later found out that he had planned to take Alex away with him! Maybe I got it wrong, but I was taught David slew Goliath, not the other way round!

Dumfounded, frustrated and tearful, I watched Alex, climb in the silver double cab, after making a strange comment to me as a farewell, "You too strong!" Whatever that was supposed to mean! Another half-baked mission trip as I saw it! All lessons on never giving up, and becoming an over-comer, God requires, and speaks of, promises for the over-comers in Revelations, chapter 2 and 3.

***

Returning to Durban held no joy for me, as I watched the love of my life, and supposed partner in ministry, turn into someone that I wasn't sure of, who I had married!

The money and energy spent back and forth to the Eastern Cape, was exhausting, but I pressed on with East London, having made contact with two other pastors in the same location but different area and organizing a hall to speak in. On arrival at the Bishop's house we were told not to go out alone, as it was a really dangerous area for themselves, let alone us as imlungus, (white people) - racism was obvious! Alex, never one to listen to such warnings or wisdom, said he hadn't got a spirit of fear and would not have anyone put one on him. He determinedly disappeared amongst the houses. Some solid, little homes, others lean-to shacks.

After some hours of no sight of Alex's return to safety, I implored the pastor to send out to look for him. My imagination, not spiritual at all, pictured having to tell his family that he was killed following Jesus and me on missions. Not being at all Christian, I could picture the outrage, as they had not even had the courtesy to meet me yet, even still today, supposedly showing their disapproval of our marriage! (Truth be known, they had got the gist of what made me tick, and refused to deal with their closet sins and roots of bitterness through family past strife!) They found Alex relaxed doing whatever with kids, and totally put out that he was indeed putting us out, as a meal had been prepared and we were to be shortly whisked away to the hall, a fair ride to travel. The most amazing moment was when I realised the hall was the very hall in Duncan Village that the volunteers from the Anastasis Mercy ship had built when I was working on the ship years previously, and I was brought out to see, and photograph, the finished building.

Then a repeat of Alex disappearing happened, the pastor said we would have to leave as he could not be held responsible for our safety. I get blamed for everything that goes wrong, rightly or wrongly so, with his insecurities of now, not having a place to stay again got the better of him. Both upset with each other, cliff hanging, on either side of the bed, trying to sleep. I had no sooner fallen asleep, that I felt Alex's hands in my hair, at first a fondness came over me, until in a flash he was dragging me up, across the bed by my hair and I could see the intent to smash me against the wall! I screamed, somehow got loose, leaving a substantial amount of hair in his hands. Without my glasses, I blindly flew down the corridor to Bishop's room, praying the door would not be locked. I knew his wife was holding an all-night prayer meeting.

Please God, don't let him have left us alone.

Bishop slept soundly, when I tried to wake him he got such a fright, the noise he made gave Alex my hiding place. Luckily Bishop reacted fast enough, getting between us, trying to calm Alex, who was threatening dire things over me! My weak shoulder joint at that moment decided to dislocate, so there was shouting from Alex still in rage, screaming from me in agony, and screaming at both of us from Bishop, was the order of the day at 2 a.m.

Bishop was not prepared to drive me to the hospital, as his wife was now due home and he said he couldn't leave her alone, so I prayerfully (for safety away from Alex) sat outside the house until dawn, nursing my arm in a position I had found, to stop the screaming pain. As daylight broke, a police van came. Bumping along the uneven, dirt road, ironically, that had been called out for a murder, two houses away! That shook Alex's ideas up! The police, kindly drove me to the hospital in East London, where I was convinced, to have a bank repair job on my shoulder, by an excellent doctor, Dr. Wait.

I soon made friends with some staff that were Christians. The one woman told me about an African evangelist that had not ministered appropriately at her church, and was demanding money. It turned out to be my Goliath, that was confirmation, he was not what he said he was, testifying that he had been a Satanist, proudly sharing the gory details, and half the church a walked out the meeting.

God had chosen not to heal my shoulder supernaturally, and I couldn't continue with the problem of it coming out of joint again, whilst I was far out, in locations or wherever. The Salvation Army in East London, kindly had Alex and I stay. While I was in hospital Alex had enough of their regime, so as soon as I was able to leave hospital, we hitched a ride to the bus depot. As Alex would say often enough, "I'm in the middle of nowhere!" He used to say that even when we stayed in a civilized European, white dominated, country village. Knowing that a town was in walking distance, he would say I had put him in the middle of nowhere! So nothing new, a complaining spirit, it seemed, never satisfied with anything particularly, unless he was being entertained at someone else's expense, with everything that cost a bomb, so he could look important! The truth told, there was no humility to that side of my dear husband!

Having a new bus company on the route, vying for customers with their new slashed fare price, was another provision from the Lord, which gave us 50 Rand to spare after paying the two tickets at 125 Rand each. On the bus a gentleman, Brian, and his daughter shared their ample prepared lunch and drinks with us, and also ministered effectively to us each individually. Thank you Jesus. Eventually as the bus pulled in, for its longest break, to Kokstad, the town considered the halfway mark to Durban, Alex, said, "I feel God says we must get off here."

My heart sank, weary with his constant bickering, his lack of cooperation in many instances, hence lack of finances. The fare we would have to pay from Kokstad to Durban would be 100 Rand, this decision seemed crazy! He had better have heard God, for his sake, if he wanted to live through my wrath. After all, my unconditional love, and long suffering forgiveness been more than I could stand, and my anger was quickly building up!

We had to drag our luggage into the tea lounge, cum restaurant, which opened onto the forefront of the very busy petrol station. The months had passed quickly, with all our backwards and forwards, and winter creeping up on us without us almost noticing. Now Kokstad's reputation as being one of the coldest places in winter was proving true! We had no choice but to purchase air-time for the phone, to call our friends, in the area, and Mt. Ayliff, which was to no avail.

The restaurant closed soon, and the adjoining hotel, even if we could afford it, was full. Alex sat thoughtfully, or prayerfully, near the fire in the centre, keeping warm. I balefully tried to find any alternatives for accommodation. When all our efforts in the natural were at and end, then there was a 'Suddenly' from our Faithful Father.

'If you will go outside, ask the driver of THAT car, to take you home with him.' God's voice said clearly.

I moved quickly as the cars did not wait around after being served. There were no cars at any of the petrol pumps, only a silver twin double cab facing the restaurant. God must mean this car. I waited, looking around for the driver. Soon an elderly man, with a typical farmer's hat perched on his head, came out the restaurant, carrying a plastic packet with take away food in. "Is this your car?" I ventured.

"Indeed it is, what can I do for you?" He replied.

"I know this might sound crazy, but I believe I heard God say I had to ask the driver of this car, to take us home with him, we are missionaries and have nowhere to stay tonight and no money"

"Well what are you waiting for, jump in"

I could hardly believe what I was hearing.

"Wait, my husband, our luggage!" I shrieked in dismay, realizing he seemed in a hurry to leave.

"Well go and fetch them!" my rescuer commanded.

Grinning widely, I woke Alex up from his awkward sleep and told him the news. Bundled in next to our new friend, we found him to be a wonderful old warrior of the cross, eagerly taking in our adventures. He explained that his wife was a master builder, and had designed their home. A beautiful log cabin complex spread out before us as we rolled up the long gravel driveway, which crunched beneath the weight of the vehicle.

It was a Bed and Breakfast, magnificently run with every convenience at hand. They settled us into a room with a king size bed, Christian Channel on the TV, and an ensuite bathroom, which was made full use of. Calling us for supper, I realized they had given us their dinner, which he had driven eight miles to get, as he had not been expecting to fetch us as well. Politely, they both showed an interest in all we had to share, giving us insights of their input into others' lives, such as ourselves. They gave us free copies of books, that one of these folk had written, full of testimonies. I mentally took note.

After a lovely evening, sleeping soundly, we were woken with the call to a homemade breakfast. Some ladies later dropped by for an informal ladies meeting, which I happily shared a little. Then the old gentleman told us that he would have to take us back to Kokstad, as he had to get on with his day.

"I hope you've done them proud?" he asked of his wife.

"That I have." she replied.

On going to say our thanks and farewells, she pressed a sealed envelope into my hands. Politeness, made me not rip it open to see God's faithfulness, but when we were alone, we shrieked with delight at the 500 Rand that was inside.

Alex had heard God, give credit where due, and I had to learn to not only trust God more, but my husband too it seemed. In some of these crises at least!

I see God training you as a mother to the oppressed, a wife to a man, a woman of God, a sister and a friend. To operate multi-dimensionally, who speaks spirit and life. You are bigger than you know, that's why many fights come to you, because the enemy is frightened of your future. As God was with Moses, so He is with you!

Prophet AARON

Lightning Source UK Ltd.
Milton Keynes UK
UKOW05014815O812

197532UK00001B/7/P

9 781906 755164